LANGUAGE AND LITERACY SERIES

Dorothy S. Strickland, FOUNDING EDITOR
Celia Genishi and Donna E. Alvermann, SERIES EDITORS
ADVISORY BOARD: *Richard Allington, Kathryn Au, Bernice Cullinan, Colette Daiute,
Anne Haas Dyson, Carole Edelsky, Mary Juzwik, Susan Lytle, Django Paris, Timothy Shanahan*

continued

For volumes in the NCRLL Collection (edited by JoBeth Allen and Donna E. Alvermann) and the Practitioners Bookshelf Series
(edited by Celia Genishi and Donna E. Alvermann), as well as other titles in this series, please visit www.tcpress.com.

–THE–
VULNERABLE HEART
OF LITERACY

Centering Trauma
as Powerful
Pedagogy

—ELIZABETH DUTRO—

Foreword by Gerald Campano / Afterword by Megan Ollett

TEACHERS COLLEGE PRESS

TEACHERS COLLEGE | COLUMBIA UNIVERSITY

NEW YORK AND LONDON

Published by Teachers College Press, 1234 Amsterdam Avenue, New York, NY 10027

Copyright © 2019 by Teachers College, Columbia University

Cover concept by Alexandra Dutro-Maeda

Library of Congress Cataloging-in-Publication Data

Names: Dutro, Elizabeth, author.
Title: The vulnerable heart of literacy : centering trauma as powerful pedagogy / Elizabeth Dutro ; Foreword by Gerald Campano ; Afterword by Megan Ollett.
Description: New York, NY : Teachers College Press, [2019] | Series: L&L series | Includes bibliographical references and index.
Identifiers: LCCN 2019023524 (print) | LCCN 2019023525 (ebook) | ISBN 9780807763131 (hardcover) | ISBN 9780807763124 (paperback) | ISBN 9780807778081 (ebook)
Subjects: LCSH: Language arts (Elementary) | Literacy—Study and teaching (Elementary) | Psychic trauma in children—Treatment.
Classification: LCC LB1576 .D88 2019 (print) | LCC LB1576 (ebook) | DDC 372.6/044—dc23
LC record available at https://lccn.loc.gov/2019023524
LC ebook record available at https://lccn.loc.gov/2019023525

ISBN 978-0-8077-6312-4 (paper)
ISBN 978-0-8077-6313-1 (hardcover)
ISBN 978-0-8077-7808-1 (ebook)

Printed on acid-free paper
Manufactured in the United States of America

Contents

Foreword

Certain kinds of trauma visited on peoples are so deep, so cruel, that unlike money, unlike vengeance, even unlike justice or rights, or the goodwill of others, only writers can translate such trauma and turn sorrow into meaning, sharpening the moral imagination.

—Morrison, 2019, p. ix

Expressions of loss, pain, yearning, and struggle require pulling other's stories into the heart and soul of shared humanity and require space to recognize the distinctions in experiences and what accounts for those differences.

—Dutro, 2019, p. 104

Reading Elizabeth Dutro's timely and courageous book, I recall a story shared with me by an immigrant-rights activist who went to schools in my city's public education system. Her family had fled to the area as refugees in the aftermath of a genocide, one which was entangled with the United States' history of imperialism. As a child, she would nurture her mother, as they frequently sat together, staring out of the window of their apartment, trying to come to grips with incomprehensible loss. In school, her teachers couldn't even find her home country on a map.

The gaping chasm between the experiences of the child at home and in school is not simply a problem of an individual teacher lacking information or even concern. Rather, it reflects a deeper crisis of ethics and of systemic hermeneutical injustices, urging us to consider the myriad of experiences, including those derived from histories of oppression, which too easily become obscured in a nation that has embraced a mythos of exceptionalism. Fanon (2008), a psychoanalyst by training, makes the useful distinction between the traumas we inevitably endure by virtue of being human, such as the unexpected death of a loved one, and the everyday indignities and suffering of colonial racism. Both kinds of traumas, often experientially inextricable, are perpetuated not only through broader political sentiments and policies, such as the ongoing state-sanctioned violence targeting immigrant families, but also through educational inequities that unevenly concentrate human precarity. I taught, for example, in an overcrowded elementary school which seemingly couldn't afford a full-time nurse or counselor, but had a significant police presence. A child in such a school may not be able to receive adequate care for a serious asthma attack or an emotional health challenge, but could be readily criminalized for a playground dispute. In classrooms, assimilationist curricula and policies promoting hyper-standardization homogenize the potential pool of hermeneutical resources for students and teachers alike, to try to make sense of a fuller range of human experience, including those that are difficult. These policies threaten to render the critical imagination vacuous.

There are current movements in education to better address socioemotional development and promote trauma-informed schooling. In sum, these initiatives reflect progress. My concern, as theorists and activists of critical disability studies have taught us, is that too often they are premised ideologically on a medical model, which locates the problem in the individual minds and bodies of students, thereby re-inscribing deficit narratives of youth and their communities. Toni Morrison reminds us, by contrast, of the potential to create new narratives out of trauma, ones that may have profound ethical implications—an endeavor of writers, poets, and artists who may be uniquely positioned to restore a fuller sense of humanity to the humanities and to education more broadly.

Elizabeth Dutro's scholarship makes an urgent intervention into current discussions of trauma and education. As a researcher who has been thinking about the intersections of trauma and literacy teaching and learning for decades, Dutro views all students themselves as writers, poets, critics, and literate beings who have the interpretive agency to make meaning out of difficult life experiences. Her book urges educators to cultivate classroom spaces where children can center, if and how they choose, stories of human fragility and loss, while also interrogating the systemic oppressions implicated in their lived experiences and how those experiences are interpreted. In foregrounding such critical witnessing alongside vulnerability, reciprocity, and care, Dutro paints a portrait of literacy invitations with "meaningful themes that allow various life stories to congregate" (p. 28). As the testimonies and actions in Dutro's carefully rendered examples of classroom life underscore, students and teachers can lead the way in sharpening our collective "moral imagination" as we work together toward a more interdependent and just world.

—Gerald Campano

Acknowledgments

The word *gratitude* can feel overused sometimes in this period of gratitude practices and journals. But each page of this book is drenched in it.

I was so lucky to work with a wonderful editor, Emily Spangler, as well as the other staff at Teachers College Press, especially Karl Nyberg, Adee Braun, and Joy Mizan. You understood what I was trying to do with this book, you valued my voice, and the book is stronger thanks to your insights. And to Gerald Campano, it is beyond an honor to have your words and presence included in this book. Thank you.

Words can't convey my appreciation for the children in Megan's classroom, as well as the other children I've had the honor of knowing over time and whose stories appear in this book. It is my immense good fortune to spend time with children who so generously shared their stories and listened to mine with such keen and caring curiosity. I'm a better human because of what children have modeled.

Megan Ollett has been friend, collaborator, and thought partner from the moment we met. Thank you for sharing your classroom—and for the passion for teaching and commitments to children that fill every corner. The book would not have been complete without your beautiful words as its close. Andrea Bien and Julia Kantor were part of our fun, caring, and committed team in taking up these inquiries with children. Later, Ellie Haberl burrowed into children's stories with me, tracing themes and listening for echoes. I'm also grateful for our inspiring team of teachers in the TREO project—Kristen Lewis, Victoria Nevarez, and Kim Melnychenko—and the teacher colleagues with whom I continue to learn in new collaborations. The leadership, faculty, staff, and students in the School of Education at CU Boulder are an extraordinarily warm, supportive, and committed group of colleagues and my writing is fueled by being part of such a positive community. In addition to those named above, a particular shout out to other former doctoral students (who all continue their impact as faculty, researchers, teachers, and writers extraordinaire): Bethy Leonardi, Sara Staley, Michael Dominguez, Subini Annamma, Makenzie Selland, Monica Gonzalez, Becky Beucher, Ashley Cartun, Cecilia Valenzuela, and Mary Kelly. Your exceptional gifts for loving, generous, lyrical, and passionately critical work have inspired me at every turn.

I'm fortunate to have BFFs who are always there with a listening ear, loving support, and wise advice. Kathleen Collins, Elham Kazemi, and Michele Moses, thanks for linking arms with me through life. And to Elizabeth Munson, my forever friend since we were 11 years old, thank you for being a memory-carrier for the whole journey.

Because I moved often in my life, home is family. I come from large clans of fierce love on both sides and I'm grateful to my grandparents, uncles, aunts, and cousins—those here and those missed—for making me part of something extraordinary. I'm so thankful for George and Amelia Maeda, who have been in my life since Daryl and I met in high school. I know Dad Maeda would be proud of me. Close families don't just happen; they are nurtured with intention and care. My parents gave that to me and my siblings. With parents like Fran and Ken Dutro, I have never had anything to add to conversations about people's frustrations with their parents. They are only unconditional love, support, and belief in me—through every step of my life. Thank you, Mom and Dad, for being the first and most important readers of this book and for generously endorsing my sharing of our family stories. I'm indebted to my baby sister Katie, who was born into a family filled with so much love and so much grief—and infused our home with joy and hope. You are the light, then and now. And to my brother, Keith, whom I deeply admire for the life he's built from harder times, I'm in awe of you. I'm so proud to be your sister. Thanks also to Joe and Briana, who prove what great taste my siblings have in partners. And, Miles and Raeah, I am a lucky auntie to have such a never-ending source of joy, snuggles, silliness, and living room dance parties.

Finally, no word for gratitude can come close to capturing what it means to share life with Daryl Maeda and Alex and Tohru Dutro-Maeda. It's like trying to describe each cell of your body. Thank you, Daryl, for being an adolescent boy with the capacity to be present for a grieving girl, and for the extraordinary partnership through every moment since. When I'm with my children, I feel the most myself. Alex and Tohru, you continually amaze and inspire me with your talents, heart, courage, and fierce commitment to justice. The year I wrote this book corresponded to a momentous time in my youngest child's life. It is an honor to be your parent, Tohru. Alex, thank you for being a sounding board and champion for my ideas as this book unfolded. And a special note of appreciation to Alex for conceptualizing potential covers for this book with such insight into the weaving of stories it contains.

This book would not exist without my younger brother, Kenny, who was my constant childhood companion and closest confidant. I wish he was here. Since that is not how our story unspooled, I'm grateful for the legacy of empathy, compassion, and connection he gifted me.

—THE—

VULNERABLE HEART
OF LITERACY

Centering Trauma
as Powerful
Pedagogy

CHAPTER 1

What Does Trauma Mean for Literacy Classrooms?

> Misery won't touch you gentle. It always leaves its thumbprints on you; sometimes it leaves them for others to see, sometimes for nobody but you to know of.
>
> —Edwidge Danticat, *The Farming of Bones*

I can't stop thinking about my great-grandmother's diary. I'm hungry to read more. I want to sit next to Mom, like we did at that mountain cabin, and decipher every word of Great-Grandma's pages. It matters when I read the diary with my mother by my side. It matters that it was over that weekend, the week of the 30th anniversary of when my little brother died. And it was Mother's Day, the Mother's Day weekend my mother needed and that the three of us made happen, her adult children. Mom and I sat close together for hours, holding the tiny diary, brown leather, delicate pages, and read aloud, not taking turns, but reading the words as soon as they made sense, words written by a woman whose formal schooling ended sometime before middle school. It is a diary of worry, fear, loss, disbelief, and loneliness. And it is weather, so much weather. And never sun. The diary is never sun, except for the implied force behind unbearable heat and, in the entries from January through May, I have to remind myself that they were written in one of the sunniest spots in one of the sunniest states. And what is happening as we read each pencil-scratched page is that a granddaughter who lost her child is reading her grandmother's account of losing her child. As a great-granddaughter, witness to a legacy of loss, immersed in unfathomable mother-mourning, I felt each page vibrate through my own grief-marrowed bones.

* * *

The hard stuff of life reverberates. One day on one of my many visits to his 3rd-grade classroom, Julian and I connected over brother loss. That spring I was crouched beside his desk, touching base on how he was doing with the writing prompt his teacher had just introduced. He kept his eyes on the pencil laying untouched on his paper. He gave a little shrug. "It's the day my baby brother died when I was 5," he shared, raising his eyes to meet mine. I dropped from my wobbly crouch to solid knees and told him how sorry I was. And then, propelled by a rush of connection, told him that the anniversary of *my* little brother's death was just 1 week away. His brother was a toddler, sick with "just the flu," like happens to all toddlers at some point. But then, inexplicably, in a moment of shrieking crib-discovery, gone. Twenty-one years before, my little brother was crushed by a falling boulder while playing with his best friend near a mountain stream. Siblings, the ones you're supposed to have along for life's ride, both of these siblings the littler ones you, the big one, are supposed to protect. They were there and then not there, in a finger-snap instant, on two wailing-siren afternoons, on days that each had dawned quietly enough. Two siblings, experiencing a moment of surprised connection at one of the many small desks, hinged lid scarred by years of surreptitious scissor gouges, as we each carved our wandering paths through the confounding wilderness of now-familiar grief.

Like Julian, many children carry deeply difficult experiences into classrooms. Like me, so do teachers. Those experiences take many forms and have varying impacts, but whether or not they are acknowledged or allowed to breathe in the official realm of curriculum, they are there. Of course we know this. We live it, see it, and hear it every day in classrooms. The everydayness of living and encountering the full range of life experiences in no way makes them less extraordinary, less arresting, less moving, less confusing. In fact, what is striking about my story of connection with Julian over our brother-loss is its profound ordinariness. It is a moment of connection over loss, which is one of those large themes of human existence that is lived, variously, but consistently, in just about any space we enter.

I'm often overwhelmed when I pause and allow myself to feel the enormity of human experience in classrooms. How can one room possibly contain it all? The joys, sorrows, open-armed greetings, and hard good-byes. So much love and disappointment. The presences and absences of so many people and places. So much pain inflicted, by others and the systems they build, nearby, far away, known and seen, or hidden from view. The hovering pasts, both haunting and comforting; the apparitional futures, shimmering with promise of beauty and threat of disaster. How can one space hold all the important tiny, mundane, and extraordinary stories of lives? The walls should burst. The windows should shatter.

Experiences of pain, sorrow, loss, fear, and disruption are an inevitable presence in schools. Each of us carries experiences across every threshold that impact how we engage with the other bodies, the objects, and the stories around us. Those lived stories are rarely apparent immediately, of course. And, they aren't always visible, audible, even after significant time together. Yet, lived experiences and the knowledge they represent are always impacting us as individuals and as a community.

As the title of this book suggests, I believe literacy provides a particularly important and bountiful context for integrating attention to challenging life experiences into our teaching. Too often, discussions about children's trauma are disconnected from the relationships and connections with others and with texts that are already ever-present in the literacies we engage with children in our classrooms. As teachers, we rarely have opportunities, whether in preservice preparation or professional development, to learn specific principles and practices to take the harder aspects of life into account in the day-to-day of our established routines of teaching and learning—and in ways that don't inflict *more* harm, create *further* marginalization.

In my collaborations with teachers and children, we've learned together how acknowledging the difficult experiences of life and supporting one another to live those experiences in schools can be mindfully woven into the process of learning with and from children. After all, literacy practices are the means through which life stories are encountered, shared, and witnessed in classrooms. Literacy classrooms are crucial contexts for engaging the complexities of trauma in classrooms. Because, for sure, it is complex. As I'll explore in this book, addressing traumas through literacies requires specific kinds of commitments, dispositions, and practices if it is to occur in ways that foster connection (and avoid alienation), honor children's choices and desires (rather than imposing an adult's agenda), and humanize children and families (rather than allowing stories we deem traumatic to exacerbate injustice). Those complexities include what counts as "trauma" and who is most likely to be deemed traumatized in schools.

Perhaps you were drawn to this book because, like me, you have experienced your own hardships. And, of course, I imagine you picked up this book with your head full of children, past and present, in your classroom who have faced a range of challenges life can wield. In addition, perhaps you, like me, have noticed increased attention to trauma as an issue in schools. I've been thinking and writing about trauma and literacy classrooms for several years and, without doubt, I have felt a geyser-eruption shift in attention toward this topic across disciplines that hold investments in trauma in relation to education.

I passionately believe we must address challenging life experiences in our classrooms. As I watch attention to trauma in schools spread, I consider how more attention to particular important aspects of children's experiences in schools has potential to result in positive impacts on resources and increased conversations across perspectives and investments. However, I need to be clear right at the outset that I am troubled by much of the policy, rhetoric, and analysis around trauma in schools. I will explore this disquiet further below, but my concerns are rooted in the flightiness of the word "trauma" and all of the complexities in how it lands on certain children. I wrote this book with the goal of keeping those complexities centered in our view as we explore how teachers can approach difficult experiences through the everyday instruction and interactions in their literacy classrooms. As we make those explorations, we'll also keep our eye on what is most important: considering how we can take up those goals in ways that honor children's lives and perspectives *and* cultivate a positive, engaged, and connected classroom community.

What happens when the far-from-easy stuff of life is acknowledged as always present in literacy classrooms and consciously made to matter in curriculum and instructional practices? We'll enter classrooms to show what can unfold when teachers committed to compassionate, critical, and equitable practice focus on that question. You'll find descriptions and illustrations of pedagogies and practices designed to provide opportunities for children to bring experiences of trauma to school literacies in positive and supported ways. Although the classroom examples are drawn from elementary classrooms, the principles I'll discuss and many of the approaches can be adapted to middle and high school contexts.

WHAT IS TRAUMA?

As a term, "trauma" is both ubiquitous in its use to describe various aspects of human experience and highly ambiguous. What counts as trauma? Who is deemed traumatized? As I imply in the discussion above, the approaches to trauma across academic disciplines is highly varied, and that variation is present in how trauma is discussed in the context of schools and schooling. From the study of literature and film, to cultural studies, to psychology, to social work, to neurology (to name but a few), researchers conceptualize and study trauma in very different ways. I discuss these approaches in more detail in Chapter 2, and throughout this book, I share my own lenses and learning on the complexities of how "trauma" arises in our lives as literacy educators. Here, we can simply absorb that there isn't consensus about the term "trauma" and what it does and should mean to children's experiences in classrooms.

When it comes to "trauma," its combination of ubiquity and ambiguity point us to two pressing issues related to trauma in classrooms:

- First, the imperative to craft classrooms that enfold children experiencing sudden or ongoing challenges in affirmation and support that are built into both the curriculum and the familiar instructional routines of literacy classrooms;
- Second, the equally necessary work of questioning what is meant by the term "trauma" and how that idea functions in relation to children, their learning, and how they are positioned in classrooms.

That first imperative requires working toward classroom practices centered on relationship, reciprocity, love, and care. It also demands eschewing practices, such as those baked into some school and classroom discipline systems, that risk isolating, targeting, and shaming children (such practices are *traumatizing* and so must be included in what counts as trauma in the context of schools and classrooms). Supporting children in the midst of challenging circumstances also means designing literacy curriculum and instructional practices that invite and value difficult experiences, rather than silencing such experiences as inappropriate for school or rendering them invisible in the texts and talk of classrooms.

At the same time, the second responsibility requires a critical stance toward both what counts as traumatic and who is deemed traumatized. Experiences interpreted as traumatic vary widely. Those experiences also can't be extricated from inequities in society and schooling. Although some difficult experiences are inevitable given fragile and finite human bodies, not all challenges are built into the human condition. Humans are very good at constructing systems and institutions that inflict difficult circumstances on some people more than others. This includes inequities related to poverty and racism, such as access to health care, housing, and quality food sources, as well as exposure to environmental risks such as lead poisoning. In addition, racism, sexism, homophobia, and xenophobia inflict risk of hardship and suffering—and, too often, overt violence—on certain children and families due to deportation, racial profiling, sexual assault, gender policing, surveillance, and overincarceration.

Literacy research explicitly focused on the complexities of trauma is growing. As one indication (and resource to check out), the widely read journal *Language Arts* recently published a themed issue on trauma, loss, and literacies that included researchers' engagements with trauma and literacies in varying contexts (Dutro, 2017; Jones & Spector, 2017; Miyazawa, 2017; Thein & Schmidt, 2017). Literacy educators have been delving into critical questions of how trauma functions in and outside of classrooms, and I urge us all to draw upon and learn from this work (e.g., Ellison, 2014; Jones, 2012; Pyscher, 2018; Wissman & Wiseman, 2011).

In addition, we know from decades of research, as well as from our own experience as educators, that many children are the target of marginalizing language and interactions in schools. Inequity and injustice, within and outside of schools, are often the *cause* of traumas and exacerbate the violence and pain inflicted on some children and families more than others (Bryant-Davis & Ocampo, 2005; Howard, 2017). Many educators have documented the ways children and youth are, to draw on the title of Olson's book, "wounded by school" (2009). Significant areas of study in literacy have engaged the impact of poverty, racism, dehumanizing immigration policies, and gender normativity and heterosexism and their intersections in students' classroom experiences (e.g., Blackburn, 2015; Campano, 2007;

Cruz, 2012; Handsfield, 2015; Jones, 2004; Jones & Vagle, 2013; Kirkland, 2013; Lewis, 2001; Valenzuela, 2010).

Why do these persistent forms of discrimination matter centrally in our considerations of trauma in literacy classrooms? As I'll explore further in Chapter 2, turning attention to trauma in children's lives risks being one more a priori assumption made about only certain children. Such patterns and risks in how trauma is defined, ascribed, and inflicted require our vigilance. As Zembylas (2008) reminds us, "trauma" in the context of schooling always has political and ethical dimensions that must be centered. But, of course, it is far from adequate to state the need for attentiveness against further marginalizing children through attention to trauma. As literacy educators, we need tools, support, and collaboration as we engage this important work.

In the midst of trauma's important complexity, we can confidently launch our exploration with the shared premise that literacy educators must approach trauma carefully, compassionately, critically, *and* centrally. My aim in the forthcoming chapters is to provide some resources, based on my experiences and learning with teacher colleagues over time, and open conversations through which we can all learn from one another. The lenses on trauma and the classroom stories I'll share show how teachers can work within trauma's complexity toward clear goals, including: inviting all aspects of lives into classrooms as source and resource for school literacies, building connected and vibrant literacy communities, advocating for students within educational systems that can be marginalizing, and ensuring that attention to trauma does not inflict additional harm on children.

To launch us toward those goals, I'll turn to a few stories that get at touchstone ideas for the deeper dives we'll take together: testimony and witness, reciprocity and vulnerability, and the extraordinary in the ordinary.

CLASSROOMS AS SITES OF TESTIMONY AND WITNESS TO TRAUMA

What does it mean to witness others' lives? Witnessing is far from straightforward. To witness is to be present, to listen, to see; yet none of those essential components ensure any benefit for the person being witnessed. And what does that person's testimony look like? Testimony to difficult experiences may be explicitly spoken or written, or may lurk implicitly in a comment during a turn and talk or in a picture drawn on the page of a writing journal; testimony may take the form of objects tucked into backpacks, an empty seat, a too-light jacket worn on a very cold day, quiet tears when the character in the story grasps her mother's hand. And because the body is always testifying to our experiences, stories of trauma are found in a quivering of lip or hand, eyes not quite focusing on a page, limbs moving oh-so-slowly across a room or squirming all the way out of chairs.

In one of the first articles I wrote on trauma and literacy, I included an account of my school experience after my brother Kenny's sudden death. I shared that, in one of those first days back at school, I fled my English class when we encountered a poem whose images, of accident and ambulance, hit too close too soon. I made it, blurry-eyed, to an empty corridor and waited for the shaking to stop. In that article, I very explicitly speak to my memory of not feeling seen, of finding no witnesses. Not a word from any classmates. No seeking out by the teacher. Just silence. That article had been in print only a short time when I attended a high school reunion and, at the requisite culminating dinner of the weekend, a classmate approached me. She held my eyes and said she remembered. And, boy did she remember, all of it, in remarkable detail—that day in English class, the poem we were reading, where she was sitting in the room, my trembling hands, my exit, the empty chair I left behind. She and I were acquainted in high school, but we weren't friends. She said she'd always wished she had followed me out, had checked on me, had told me how sorry she was. She didn't. But she had been a witness to my experience in a way I had never imagined. She didn't say it explicitly, but I came away from our reunion conversation with the clear sense that she had held *her* experience of witnessing *my* experience in a deep way, a way that couldn't help but impact how she approached others she encountered. Even after more than 20 years, her witnessing mattered. It mattered to me and it seemed to matter to her.

On the day I fled that classroom, the onus, I imagine we agree, was not on my classmate to take the actions or say the words she later regretted not taking or saying. The responsibility, though, was on my teacher. Over the years, I've been disturbed by the number of conversations I've had with kids who have experienced trauma—an unfathomable loss of person, home, innocence, security, or safety—who share very matter-of-factly that many adults in school never mentioned it. Of course, there are stories of adults who did, but the silence and avoidance are deafening in many children's accounts. I liked to think that my experience was an anomaly. I can think of just two adults in school—the principal and one teacher—who spoke to me about my suddenly upended life. The principal's support, his seeing of me and what I was experiencing, was persistent and ongoing—checking in, seeking out, inviting into conversation, communicating with my parents to extend support to my family. It was appreciated at the time. In hindsight, it was remarkable.

The teacher who spoke to me explicitly—a brief but impactful inter-action after class that first day back—was the teacher with whom I would have said I had the least connection. To say that we lacked relationship is a huge understatement. Mr. Forester, the chemistry teacher who seemed to never smile and, in my view, held no patience for the lab-lost and confused sorts like me, was a teacher to whom I had never spoken, not one word. As I stacked my books to leave class that day, he said, "Beth, could you stay a moment?" He looked me in the eye and said he was so sorry to hear about my brother. I must have said thank you, and then I left. I didn't know until soon after that encounter that Mr. Forester had lost his daughter to a vicious and notorious serial killer many years before. In my interpretation now, that horrific fact of his life is deeply connected to this usually distant teacher's request that I linger after his class that day.

These linked experiences gave me a lot to contemplate about witnessing others' lives. What counts as witnessing in classrooms? What forms does testimony take? How might we cultivate a spirit of witnessing in the literacies we engage in with children? How can we weave opportunities for testimony and witnessing seamlessly into the texts, lessons, talk, writing, and sharing that are part and parcel of our work as literacy teachers? How might we craft our classrooms in ways that help children feel seen and held in the midst of the challenges they face? How do we infuse witnessing with the knowledge that the stakes are higher for some children than others in how their life experiences are heard and interpreted by adults with power? How can witnessing be infused with advocacy, love, and fierce commitment to justice? What must we do in light of the life stories lived in our classrooms? In my work with teachers and children, these questions have fueled the idea of *critical witness* as a pillar of considering trauma in classrooms.

Vulnerability and Reciprocity

The vulnerability of children, at the mercy of powerful adults as they most often are, is overwhelming. I write this in 2018 in the United States, when the inhumanity of government toward children is starkly on display with the forced separation of families on the country's southern border. Cruelty aimed at children, trauma cultivated so overtly, is always present, of course, but sometimes, like at this moment in history, it is on neon-bright display.

Vulnerability is a crucial ingredient in the pedagogies I'll discuss in this book. As I have experienced over and over, children are so often generous with the benefits of the doubt they give to the adults they encounter in schools. This generosity lives alongside the reality that way too often children's life stories are held against them in schools. We'll see the ways children navigate vulnerability in their literacies, even as so much of what is exposed about them is beyond their control (those cumulative files just get thicker over their years in school). *Teachers'* vulnerability to children, though, needs intentional cultivation. Thus, reciprocity is key to harnessing vulnerability as an intentional and powerful practice in literacy classrooms. Children's willingness to *try* to trust makes any lack of reciprocal vulnerability all the more dismaying. This is one key reason I share some of the most important experiences of my life with students, including my deepest sorrows, raw moments, the jagged edges, and the tender spots. Vulnerability can be the path to connection in ways that allow the hardest parts of life to reside in classrooms. It's not easy to perform vulnerable teaching, that's for sure. As Elizabeth Johnson (2014) reminds us, "Vulnerability of others illuminates our own vulnerability" (p. 583), and that is sometimes far from comfortable. Educators have written beautifully about how powerful practice can arise when teachers embrace vulnerability by sharing their own life narratives with students (e.g., Johnson, 2017; Vagle & Jones, 2012). Reciprocity, too, is the stuff of powerful prose by literacy researchers. Jackson, Sealey-Ruiz, and Watson (2014) write of "reciprocal love" in working with students as "an understanding that a love for the self is inextricably linked to a love for others; an acknowledgment that good ground produces good fruit, which in turn produces good seed to be sown in good ground in an endless cycle of regeneration" (p. 399). They remind us that it is love we are aiming for in this work. While the consequences of my vulnerability in the classroom are not comparable to students', how can I ask children to take those risks if I'm not willing to?

Addressing Trauma in Everyday Teaching and Learning

Life's hardships are never routine. In an important way, the experiences we view as traumatic should resist our comprehension, spark uncertainty, and prompt self-doubt. What does this child's experience require? How can I possibly be up to the task? Such self-questioning is inevitable and important. Such questions, though, must be challenged. Because the word trauma holds such ambiguity and such weight, it can feel as though it has to be approached only by specialists or, at the least, with specialness. Visualize approaching "trauma." Many images may come to mind. Perhaps you imagine donning a surgeon's gown, hands held aloft, freshly sterilized, waiting for someone to place the gloves, tie the mask (for me, that surgeon is definitely Christina from *Grey's Anatomy*); then there is the approach toward the traumatized body, and, finally, the immense-stakes-filled handling of whatever that word, trauma, is describing. In that vision, the person standing under those bright lights sure better have had those years and years of preparation. What could be scarier than imagining someone in that vision (like me and, probably, you!) without highly specialized training?

Or, perhaps, for some of us, a more apt image is of being asked to carry an inconceivably expensive, irreplaceable, thin-glassed artist's creation across an icy pond. Who would possibly volunteer for or accept such a mission? Who wouldn't want to slink away to the back of the crowd or turn and run for the hills? Such a task should only go to the person specially prepared—crampons on the boots, clingy rubber gloves, and experience traversing frozen surfaces. Whatever the image, the result is avoidance and, in these analogies, perfectly justified and responsible evasion.

However, engaging with children in powerful, visceral, critical literacies that invite the difficult aspects of children's (and teachers') lives into classrooms in rich and supportive ways is not something we have to imbue with quite those stakes. If we do, I can't imagine how we'd ever risk the connections, the witnessing, that human lives require in our classrooms. Whether acknowledged or lurking under the surface, the images and metaphors we hold around a word like trauma matter in how we consider its presence in classrooms. If we ascribe such specialness and specialization to witnessing children's lives and making experiences truly count as part of what it means to be invited into a literacy learning community, trauma becomes bracketed from the everyday of teaching and learning. So it is imperative we consider different images, alternate metaphors. I'll turn to just one example that feels much more productive to me and gets to the heart of what I'll be exploring in these pages.

At times throughout my life, I've had a chance to be around recently hatched baby chicks. And when invited to hold one, I don't hesitate—I didn't as a 5-year-old and I don't now. I step up and hold my hands out, cupped and ready to cradle the tiny, fragile, cheeping ball of yellow fluff. My heart leaps a little with what it will require—care, gentleness, keen attention. It is a moment suffused with responsibility. Yet with some coaching and support from those who surround me, even 5-year-old me can step up, willingly, and nurture, not harm. And given the chance, I could do that every day. Each time would require the exact same measure of care and attention. But it would, at the same time, become more familiar, something I could come to expect and assume as part of my everyday experience.

Now at this point in my description of this metaphor it may seem pretty clear what the chick represents. But let me be clear, children who have experienced trauma are *not* the baby chick. The chick is the difficult experiences that anyone in the classroom community carries into that shared space. To position children as the fragile creature is central to the problem with how trauma might be approached. Viewing *children* as the chick implies an adult as the only participant with agency; an adult who, in this metaphor, is not only literally much larger, but also looms largest as the protagonist in the story. One reason I include my 5-year-old self in this image is to emphasize children as active subjects here. The children, and the teacher, are the hands that gently, but without trepidation, cradle the stories in their classroom.

To bring this image to our focus here, addressing trauma can be integrated into the ongoing relationships and instructional routines of literacy classrooms. Why is it important to approach difficult life experiences as part and parcel of the instructional routines and activities that already exist in our literacy classrooms? A key reason relates to the various images I presented above of surgeons, irreplaceable objects, and fragile, breathing fluff balls. The alternative to attending to difficult life experience as an ongoing, vital, and vibrant process in classrooms is that what is deemed traumatic becomes rarified. As a result, the idea of "addressing trauma" can be relegated to a distinct planned event or a periodic isolated activity that requires some equivalent of that pre-surgery process.

And here is where I share a central argument that I bring to these pages: Relegating, isolating, or evading certain life experiences in classrooms relegates, isolates, or evades certain *children* in literacy classrooms. No one wishes for that to be the case for any child in our care. What we want is for children to feel central, included, seen, and heard. Yet we know (from research, as well as our own experiences and observations) that certain life experiences, including many deemed traumatic, are pushed to the margins or entirely off the page in the everyday routines of literacy classrooms. In other words, in my experience, the stakes for children, and for teachers, are higher in avoidance than they are in immersion. But of course it is not a straightforward project to make the difficult aspects of life matter in ways that support the child—as a person and as a learner who deserves rich and connected opportunities to engage with literacies. We need tangible and actionable practices, as well as resources and collaboration, to support principles and commitments crucial to bringing those practices to our teaching in ways that serve children well. We get to explore those practices and resources in detail as we head into the chapters that follow.

CONTEXTS AND IDEAS WE'LL EXPLORE

As this book unfolds, I'll share experiences and examples of literacy instruction and children's work from several elementary classrooms, from 2nd through 5th grades. My role in these classrooms ranged from classroom teacher to university-based researcher. My memories of the children I taught are viscerally present as I pursue the questions that fuel this book, and they appear periodically throughout these pages. I draw most centrally on what I've learned from children and teacher colleagues in my role as researcher over the last 20 years. One of the joys of my work life is the gift of spending significant time in classrooms, building relationships with children, and participating actively in the life of the classroom as I collaborate with teacher colleagues on inquiries about shared interests.

Although I'll share stories from my own life and teaching, from Marie's 3rd-grade classroom, and from some other teacher colleagues' classrooms, we'll get to know Megan's 2nd-grade classroom the most deeply. Megan and I spent 3 years designing and documenting literacy practices that engaged with trauma in ways we came to experience as productive, connective, and critical. Two colleagues, Andrea and Julia, who were doctoral students at that time, were valued collaborators in this study. Megan's classroom was a central space in which the pedagogies of testimony and critical witness I introduce, unpack, and illustrate in the coming chapters were designed, honed, and studied.

Each chapter in this book draws on the stories and voices of children and teachers to burrow more deeply into the questions and ideas surrounding trauma and the literacy classrooms I've touched on here (and all children's names are pseudonyms). Chapter 2 will explore and illustrate the three central tenets of a pedagogy of testimony and critical witness. I'll unpack the key concepts of reciprocity, testimony, and critical witness; the ideas that underlie them; and how they function together. I'll turn to stories of teachers and children to help bring them to life.

Chapter 3 follows closely on Chapter 2 to show how pedagogies of testimony and witness were taken up in Megan's classroom in the first year of our work together. This chapter will follow the journey of Megan and her students to show how she integrated these pedagogies into the instructional contexts and routines of her literacy instruction. As part of this exploration of these pedagogies, my goal is to provide opportunities to consider how the skills and strategies of literacy lessons and standards-based, district-mandated curricula can be harnessed to positively and productively integrate attention to challenging, traumatic life experiences into the ongoing practices and relationships of the literacy classroom.

Chapter 4 focuses on genre instruction as a context for addressing trauma. We'll explore how to weave testimony and critical witness to trauma into genre units typically taught in the elementary literacy classroom, including poetry, letter-writing, and informational and narrative genres. Each genre discussion is illustrated with student work, as well as excerpts from lessons in which a teacher planned for testimony and critical witness, while centrally addressing grade-level standards.

A key finding from our study of pedagogies and practices addressing trauma is that we can trace children's testimonies to trauma across genres and across the school year. Chapter 5 shares stories from the lives and literacies of children as they engaged with pedagogies of testimony and critical witness across their school years. Each child we'll follow had experienced trauma—death of loved ones through illness, accident, or violence; separation or threat of separation from family via parental separation or divorce, incarceration, deportation, child protective services, and/or the foster care system; and loss of stable housing or living situations. We'll see how the intentional take-up of pedagogies of testimony and critical witness across a school year invites children to integrate their difficult experiences and the knowledge they've gleaned from their lives into their school literacies, in both subtle and explicit ways.

The conclusion, Chapter 6, ties the preceding chapters together to emphasize why pedagogies of testimony and critical witness are powerful for all children's literacy learning. The final chapter reiterates the key stances and strategies we can immediately take up in our teaching to ensure that difficult life experiences are honored and made to count as resources for literacy learning and as contexts for deep human connection and advocacy. I also turn to how teachers can navigate their own well-being, find networks of support, and engage in the work of compassionately and critically integrating trauma into their literacy instruction. We know we must bring open hearts, vulnerability, and fierce analysis and advocacy to this work with children. However, educators also need support and advocacy in these efforts to honor children's and their own challenging experiences.

As we proceed, I need to make it crystal-clear that what I explore on these pages is inextricably connected to the powerful and beautiful work others have done that I have had the privilege of reading, hearing, watching, and thinking about over many years. I write into long traditions of thoughtful people doing necessary and transformative work—on the page, in schools and classrooms, and in communities. To cite all of these veins of connection would fill another book, but in the words of the scholars that I have threaded into the chapters and the resources on the website connected to this book (elizabethdutro.com), you will find examples of those arteries that can send you further into the heart of stories of classrooms, teachers, and children that will enrich your life and teaching.

Finally, one more note on a decision I made during the process of writing: I decided to transcribe children's writing with conventional spelling and punctuation. Why do that? I know from my research and others' that conventions of grammar and spelling are hard for adults to bracket when attempting to see, hear, and feel children's ideas, meaning, lovely turns of phrase, and vivid images (Dutro, Selland, & Bien, 2013). The focus of this book is on the content of children's literacies in the context of their lives, so accessing their meaning is our paramount goal.

I have no doubt that some of the ideas I've explored in this first chapter are familiar in feeling, if not in name. Ideas like *critical witness*, challenging *deficit perspectives* that inflict harm on children, the use and presence of *testimony* as integral to what happens in literacy classrooms, *reciprocity* in revealing what matters most in life, and the heart-piercing *connections and punctuating moments* in any given school day—these are things teachers sense, stumble upon, glimpse, or follow like a giddy toddler chasing a firefly. And, for sure, these are pedagogies we can craft with intention.

FOR REFLECTION, DISCUSSION, AND PRACTICE

- What are the images and metaphors that come to mind when you think about trauma in relation to schools and classrooms and your role in addressing trauma?

- What is a difficult experience you carry? How has it shaped who you are in the world? How has it impacted your relationships with others (whether or not that experience is ever shared or spoken)? When, if ever, do you find that experience coming up for you in your professional life?

CHAPTER 2

Pedagogies of Testimony and Critical Witness in the Literacy Classroom

In those days and weeks after my brother died, I remember feeling both caught in the vortex and watching its funnel-swirl from the edge. I was feeling all that a body could possibly feel and I was watching two other people, the backbones of my life, feeling something incomprehensible to me. I had been nearby, at the top of the hill, right after that steamrolling rock hit my brother. We were spending the weekend on that dry-forested western mountain, and when people first began to gather to peer over the edge of the bluff to the small, winding brook below, I thought they must have seen a deer or maybe even a bear. I moved with curiosity toward the abyss. The ambulance came, but wasn't needed, because it was a helicopter that rushed him from mountainside to emergency room. The rest is a grainy, muted film, like a nightmare version of those Super 8 home movies that my parents took of the two of us when we were small—holding hands at the Grand Canyon, waving excitedly in front of Christmas trees, running wildly together in some long-forgotten front yard. The frantic drive down the mountain; the glimpse of my brother's face, unrecognizable, as we gathered in his room before being hastily ushered away; and, by nightfall, the unspeakable news. And then the drive home, the three of us in the backseat of some friend's car, my mother clutching the pill bottle the doctor had given her, just enough pills for each of my parents to sleep that night and not one pill more. We'd just arrived home when my mother paused at the closet where his jacket hung and she was uncomprehending, all body shaking and small, animal sounds. It was tears and terror, and, in my movie-reel memory, she sobs something about emptiness and no way forward and I whisper, a child's voice, a child's question, "Will we ever go out for ice cream again?"

* * *

Megan touched Dimitri's shoulder as she crouched by his desk, ready to confer with him about his writing. His writer's notebook was open, but the page was blank. It was the third week of 2nd grade and the class had just read the book *Courage* by Bernard Weber. Megan had chosen this book to share early in the year because more than one of her students was facing circumstances that required courage. As she introduced the book, she explained, "I chose this book because I love it. When my sister went to college, I gave it to her. That can be a scary time, because you're away from your family for the first time." She told the children that they could be thinking of connections as they listened. "What was a time when you had courage, when you were brave?" After she finished the story, she said, "Close your eyes and think of a time you were really brave." Courage, she explained, doesn't mean you're not afraid, but that you had to face something even though you *were* afraid.

Megan voiced some ideas about connections the children might make—doing something alone for the first time; having to face something or someone even though you are scared; the fear you experience when you or someone you love is hurt, sick, or has to go to the hospital. The children had shared their ideas with each other in a turn and talk and, now, each child was drafting ideas for a personal narrative about a time they were brave or showed courage. "Do you know what you want to write about?" Megan asked Dimitri. He nodded but looked hesitantly from his notebook to his teacher. "I know what I want to write about, but it's not for school," he whispered. Megan was pretty sure she knew the experience at the heart of Dimitri's dilemma. She had looped with him and most of his classmates from 1st to 2nd grade and vividly remembered hearing about Dimitri's grandfather's suicide the previous year. As she sat with him, the blank page between them, she remembers telling him, "It's okay. If you want to write about it in our classroom, you can write about it. It's an important part of your life." Dimitri then told Megan about the moment his mom had come to tell him that his grandfather had shot himself. He then put his story on the page for the first, but not the last, time that year.

So often, children who have experienced trauma face a conundrum. Dimitri senses that this salient, traumatic, crucial event from his life—the experience he was most compelled to bring to his writing—might not be welcome in school literacies. At the same time, if he would accept an invitation to bring that experience into school, he gets no guarantees it will be met with privacy, empathy, compassion, and critical advocacy. What can we do to ensure that we are the teachers who can offer Dimitri those invitations *and* make Dimitri those assurances?

Of course, no magic formulas exist for negotiating the complexities of human lives coming together in a shared space of connection and learning. There can't be, as those lives are so variously impacted by social forces, personal circumstances, power in all its forms, *and* just plain human fragility. Yet we can make moves and cultivate mindsets that impact children's opportunities to bring the fullness of their lives, including trauma, to bear on school literacies. Toward that end, in this chapter I first turn to the complex territory of trauma and education right now and explore why it requires such careful navigation. I then introduce and explore *pedagogies of testimony and critical witness:* the approach, mentioned in the previous chapter, that our teacher inquiry team crafted in our study of trauma as part of the everyday teaching, learning, and relationships in classrooms. Those pedagogies are grounded in three central tenets that capture the interwoven commitments and intentional moves that we found powerful as routes for children to employ their experiences of trauma as sources of connection and learning in the literacy classroom. In my experience, these ideas, tied to actions, are crucial and impactful in acknowledging trauma as an important presence in literacy classrooms and honoring children experiencing challenges. For each, I turn to classroom examples and teachers' voices to illustrate what it means, how it can be enacted in your practice, and why it matters.

NAVIGATING APPROACHES TO TRAUMA IN EDUCATION

In education, movements, interventions, approaches—whatever we call them—have this way of swooping in and, before we know it, we see them everywhere we turn. I feel this way about the expanding landscape of "trauma-focused," "trauma-sensitive," and "trauma-informed" schools. My intent here is not to systematically review or go deep into all of the examples of those approaches. Instead, I will zoom out to try to convey why I think this landscape of trauma in schools requires very careful navigation. I am not arguing to dismiss programs focused on trauma-informed schools. Not at all. For one thing, they are quite varied. For another thing, all of these proliferating programs, books, and articles on trauma's presence in children's lives and learning in schools and classrooms have at least one thing in common: All are crafted from well-meaning and compassionate intentions. The call to take seriously the experiences children bring to school permeates this movement.

I am making a case, though, for bringing a discerning eye and questioning stance to those programs. My concerns fall into roughly two areas. For one, the emphasis on medical, biological, and cognitive impacts of trauma can position children as damaged. Second, teachers are often positioned as healers in these approaches, while children are the wounded. I briefly unpack each of these concerns below so we can have them in mind as we turn to literacy classrooms.

What Is the Risk of Focusing on Neurobiological Impacts?

In many of the approaches to trauma designed for professional development, teachers are immersed in a swirl of forms of evidence and interventions—medical, psychological, clinical, and interpersonal. The emphasis on biological and clinical dimensions of trauma is part of what we have to navigate. Here's my worry: No matter how positive the intention, an emphasis on how trauma damages children makes it difficult to see the whole child, including the knowledge, empathy, and wisdom about life that children bring to their learning.

When you search "trauma and schools," you see many examples of programs and research designed to understand and address cognitive and behavioral impacts of trauma on children's learning. In addition to the explicitly medical and clinical discussions of trauma's impact on children, there are many organizations, programs, scholars, and educators situated outside of the health sciences that draw on medical and psychological brain research as rationale, explanation, or framework for the kinds of interventions and practices they advocate.

In medicalized arguments about trauma and its impacts, traumatic experiences may serve as evidence of damage that requires healing and/or remain bound tightly to "cognitive effects" based on brain-based research. Some programs and approaches involve extracurricular group and individual supports for students assessed to be impacted by trauma, while others call for trauma-informed practices to be infused across the curriculum and contexts of classrooms and schools (e.g., Souers & Hall, 2016). Some authors and organizations focus primarily on schools and school staff, whereas others very explicitly involve parents, families, and communities (e.g., WestEd, 2015). Some educational psychologists may emphasize the neurological effects of trauma on children's development, while also attending to school community, climate, and care (e.g., Craig, 2015). Authors situated in social work may point to the need to develop resilience in children in light of the traumas they have experienced (e.g., Souers & Hall, 2016). A decades-long organization, the Trauma and Learning Policy Initiative (TLPI), founded in Massachusetts in the 1990s, draws from multiple disciplines and generates extensive resources for schools (traumasensitiveschools.org). Duncan-Andrade (2011), a scholar of critical studies of race and racism in schooling and pedagogy, situates the neurobiological impact of trauma on children and youth around longstanding policies that have systematically oppressed communities of color in the city neighborhoods in which he locates his work.

These are just some of the programs and perspectives in play on issues of trauma, children, and schools. It's a lot for teachers to traverse, for sure, and the stakes are high in how we pick our way through this tricky terrain. Is any of this unimportant? No. BUT, if mis- or overused in relation to children in schools, a neurobiological, medical lens risks quickly and inappropriately pathologizing children or families.

Who Is "Well" and Who Is "Wounded"?

It is striking that almost all of the models and metaphors surrounding trauma's impact on children and their schooling implicitly or explicitly create a dichotomy between the traumatized child and the un-traumatized adult supporting them in schools. The word "healer" may not always be explicitly used in relation to adult educators in these conversations, but it is often implicit. *Healing* and *healer* are words we can't disentangle from medical and therapeutic contexts. I'm so struck by how the one category (the well adult positioned to help heal the child) creates the other category as an opposite (the damaged child in need of healing). Again, it is not that we, as caring adult educators, cannot craft classrooms and relationships in which children feel nurtured and held in bringing pain, fear, and sorrow to life and learning while in school. We can! Considering, with teacher colleagues (with you!), how to craft those classrooms is a primary focus of my professional life. However, it matters how we frame those aims because it never works to a child's advantage to create yet another form of us/them division. Words, pictures, images of brain scans, statistics—they pile up and construct binaries that will always risk fueling the deficit perspectives that already impact opportunity and well-being for children of color and those facing poverty. (Similar arguments have been made about the focus on "grit" in schools; see Blad, 2015, and Strauss, 2014, for interesting discussions).

Variations on Maslow's Hierarchy of Needs is another metaphor, a visual one this time, that is quite common in discussions of trauma in schools. To say at this point in history that many social science researchers have rejected that triangular model of "self-actualization" is an understatement. Yet versions of it persist as evidence in discussions of trauma and children in schools. For instance, I was struck in reading Forbes's (2012) work on children's trauma in schools that Maslow's hierarchy was so prominent. She adapts the Maslow's pyramid to focus on learning and writes that "this single graphic is a reflection of the entire contents of this book" (p. 6). The change in education, she argues, needs to focus on the bottom layers of the pyramid, physiological and safety needs, or learning cannot occur for some children. Now let me be clear that, although I have my critiques, her work advocates for some changes in schools that I strongly support, including removing discipline systems that target certain children and cultivating strong and loving relationships in classrooms, among other important recommendations. So what do I find so troubling about such a strong focus on a triangular vision of who is ready for learning? After all, it's not that basic needs of food, shelter, love, and security are unimportant. Those needs are beyond important and are at the top of our most longed-for wish list for each and every child. It is the case, though, that a graphic representation of "levels" and "stages" imposes its own logic on us, even when some of what we're seeing with our own eyes and hearing with our own ears defies the logic of that representation. This also goes for other pyramid representations of the consequences of trauma that you may encounter, in which the bottom level means you got lucky and the top means you're at risk for early death. The bottom line is that these pyramids didn't grow in nature; they weren't plucked from a branch, already formed. These are human-constructed hierarchies.

All of this makes me think of William, who entered my 2nd-grade classroom in my first year of teaching. I knew that William was having a particularly chaotic experience at home that November. Neighbors' calls to the police when the sounds from the house turned from shouts to screams had prompted the involvement of child protective services. With frequent visits from a social worker, William was still at home with his mom, but the boyfriend had been told not to return to the house and a restraining order was in process. I'd seen the red-faced anger come quicker over the weeks, but he responded well to my redirecting, kneeling beside him, clasping his hands in mine, and looking into his eyes with whispered reassurances that his turn with that particular book would come again quickly, or that it was just next week when it would be his turn to feed our class rats, Fievel and Gus. Then came the day when William threw his chair right in the middle of our literacy block, not hitting any children but coming too close. Everyone froze, and I tried to calm the quiver in my voice as I waved my hands toward a corner of the room and told the other children to quickly gather there. I stood between William and the huddled children. William let out a howl from the core of his little body, eyes shut tight. I'm right here, William, I whispered to him as I walked to him. William, that sweet child, who loved himself a Shel Silverstein poem, turned balled fists to shuddering tears as I wrapped my arms around him while softly talking one of his classmates through the process of calling the school office and asking the Assistant Principal to come to our classroom.

Yes, William needed all the resources we could muster in our school—which were, frankly, not nearly adequate at that place and time. Yes, his family's situation was on the radar of counselors and other professionals in the ways required by both law and ethics. Yes, as his teacher, the onus was on me to advocate for those supports to the best of my ability (also inadequate, even as I know my very young self was trying). What William did *not* need from me, his teacher? He did not need me to see him as broken. He did not need me to impose a pre-existing framework onto his complex life in a way that defined him as damaged, made him someone unable to learn.

How Do Life Experiences Enter and Circulate in Classrooms?

Reading broadly on ideas of trauma and schools, a few things became quite clear: What counts as trauma is ambiguous; who is deemed traumatized is troubling; and, in locating the damage of trauma, evidence and frameworks construct binaries that can so quickly (and wrongly) be solidified as "real." So, years ago, when I turned the focus of my research to trauma and literacy classrooms, I sought voices and frameworks from cultural and literary theorists, including feminist writers, scholars of color, and LGBTQ authors who were pushing scholarship to question long-held assumptions and attune to voices and perspectives that had long been excluded. These were areas of research and writing central to my scholarship that had always helped me keep critical questions in view. Who benefits from this? Whose perspectives are being heard and honored here? How is the world being divided in this language in ways that benefit some more than others? What is being made invisible? Who and what is the subject of this language—and who and what is the object? What needs to be questioned and resisted in the way this is being "sold" to me? These are important questions for many issues in education, and all the more so for something like trauma that is so tied to medical and neurological language that feels so definitive.

Searching for a language that felt adequate to express the importance of the difficult stories that students brought to literacy classrooms and the complexity of how those stories are taken up in schools, I turned to trauma studies. Trauma studies researchers in the humanities disciplines examine the presence and role of trauma in literature, film, and significant historical events and grapple with the inadequacy of language to represent traumatic events. This spoke to me and my experiences as an educator and researcher in elementary classrooms. I knew very well that a range of challenging experiences always lived in classrooms. I wanted to better understand how those experiences *circulated* in classrooms. I knew that those experiences were consequential for children, but I wanted to know more about *how* those stories were consequential for children. Classrooms, we know, are high-stakes gathering places for children. I wanted to think about how attending closely to difficult experiences in literacy classrooms could bring insights into how narratives of human lives function in spaces where people come together (Hartman, 1995, p. 554).

Reframing Responses to Trauma

William was struggling, and for good reason. He was responding to his circumstances in ways that made sense. Picture it, what a visual like Maslow's pyramid does to us. In that one, you're at or near the top, right? My sense is that most of us on the receiving end of those particular approaches to children's trauma are assumed to be in that top level of that triangle. As William is ushered into the large basement of that structure, I can't even see him from this penthouse of actualization I've been gifted. I may not have thrown furniture, but my own raw raging at the world was a fresh memory the year William threw his chair—my closed-car-window screams, the clenched-fist fingernails cutting into my soft palm flesh. Yet, as always, the view is great from the high perch that I did nothing to earn but be White and economically secure. As for those other pyramids specific to trauma that also show up on slides, where the ground floor is the ideal place to be? No one has evaluated me, I'm pretty sure, through those middle layers, where I'd belong, with their frightening predictions for my life. William and so many children know more than I can ever know; they skillfully navigate layers of life and its injustices in ways I can only watch and vow to learn from; they capture in their literacies an image, a heart-skipping turn of phrase I have never encountered before or since.

I'm convinced that it doesn't matter that these hierarchical approaches to children's trauma are "just a helpful metaphor" or a "limited, but productive way of seeing the impacts of trauma" (phrases I have heard more than once). Those images, metaphors, and frameworks label children as damaged, broken, wounded; and they construct teachers as the unbroken, the healthy healers. Historian and trauma studies scholar Dominick LaCapra (2001) captures this well, writing "the binary opposition is very closely related to the scapegoat mechanism . . . so that the other becomes totally different [from the self]" (p. 149). Those us/them binaries that some popular images and frameworks create chip away at children's humanity. Teachers can support children experiencing trauma without positioning them through those lenses. We can choose to reject and revise those pervasive narratives. We can bring our questions to approaches to trauma and do our own dissecting of what will serve us and children well and what assumptions need to be unearthed and challenged. We can consciously reframe the assumptions of who needs healing and who is wounded (Dutro, 2011; Frank, 2013). We can attend to the difficult dimensions of life as a reciprocal, circular, and ever-present process in literacy classrooms.

TENETS OF PEDAGOGIES OF TESTIMONY AND CRITICAL WITNESS

In this section, I describe three tenets of pedagogies of testimony and critical witness that teacher colleagues and I came to over time: 1) Testimony and Witness are reciprocal; 2) Critical Witness requires action and advocacy; 3) Testimony and Critical Witness to trauma are woven into the fabric of school literacies. First, though, I turn to the terms "testimony" and "witness" and how I'm using them. and then discuss the three tenets that capture the central ideas of these pedagogies.

Testimony and witness are central terms in the field of trauma studies, especially in scholarship in the humanities disciplines, like English, Comparative Literature, and Cultural Studies. I've been captivated by those words since I started pursuing work focused on trauma and literacies. They each hold varied shades of meaning, appear in wide-ranging places, and conjure multiple images. Testimony and witness are also tangled up with one another. As just one example, people called "witnesses" provide testimony to what *they've* witnessed; their testimony is witnessed by juries in the courtroom. They are paired in that room; one doesn't make sense without the other. Those courtroom contexts, though, put capital-letter expectations on Testimony and Witness. There, they loom large and the height of the stakes is clear. But we can also see the high stakes in the everyday, small ways that people around us are testifying to their experiences and witnessing others' lives.

Testimony is attesting to an experience and, in the dictionary, it is defined as a "formal" spoken or written accounting of an event. For our purposes, we get to expand what is recognized as testimony into all the ways the human body and the objects surrounding it might attest to what that person is and has been through: a quiet sigh, a gouged table top, a turned back, an overturned chair, a book hidden on a lap, a playground push, a sudden sob, a door slam punctuating the flee from the room. A child's testimony to trauma takes so many forms, as does our own.

Before we get too far into a discussion of testimony, I want to highlight "testimonio" as an important form of storytelling with roots in Latin American indigenous communities. When a person of color shares a story of experience, a testimonio, their story speaks to the impacts of colonization, racism, and other intersecting forms of marginalization (González, Plata, García, Torres, & Urrieta, 2003; Saavedra, 2019). Put another way, in testimonio, a story of personal experience also signals the larger histories of oppression to which it is connected. As this book unfolds, we'll see children of color sharing their experiences in ways that serve as testimonio. For instance, when Lara writes of her uncle's deportation and its ripple effects on her family, her story is inseparable from the histories of racism and fear-mongering surrounding the policies and rhetoric of immigration in the United States. Teachers have taken up testimonio in literacy classrooms in ways that richly support children to bring their knowledge to their school literacies (including their emerging political understandings) and that expose the consequences of marginalization and deficit perspectives in schools (e.g., DeNicolo & Gonzalez, 2015; Ghiso & Low, 2013; Handsfield & Valente, 2016; Pacheco, 2009). For some excellent examples of testimonio in classrooms, see the list I include on the book website (elizabethdutro.com).

Given the rich histories of testimonio, why did I opt to use the term "testimony" in this book? Testimonio has a specific and crucial meaning connected to forms of racial oppression, so I need to be careful not to appropriate the term for any and all stories of experience, no matter how impactful those experiences may be. As a White educator, for example, my stories of experience are not testimonios. When using the term testimonio, it matters *who* is sharing their story. As we go forward, let's hold onto the idea that *some* stories we'll encounter are children's testimonios to the inequities impacting their lives, while *all* of the children's experiences serve as testimony.

THREE TENETS OF PEDAGOGIES OF TESTIMONY AND CRITICAL WITNESS

Tenet One: Testimony and Witness Are Reciprocal. Teachers model and engage in the risk and vulnerability of bringing difficult experiences into the public space of classrooms, a risk that too often falls only on students. Thus, teachers first position students as their witnesses and, at the same time, their own sharing serves as invitation and sanction for drawing on deeply felt life experiences as source and resource for school literacies, including those that would be characterized as difficult. For instance, in a mini-lesson on organization of personal narrative, Megan purposely focuses her modeled writing on the day she learned of her grandfather's death. At the end of the mini-lesson, children are invited to write stories that matter to *them*. But by inviting children to witness a significant experience in her life, loss is explicitly included in what counts in school writing.

Tenet Two: Critical Witness Requires Action and Advocacy. Serving as critical witnesses for students requires recognizing both the deep connections provided by shared human experience and also the power differentials and social inequities that can result in very different consequences for how teachers and students are positioned by the life stories narrated by themselves or others. Critical witness, then, involves actively working to engage in critical analyses of the deficit discourses surrounding many students and public education and taking steps to advocate for students and work toward social justice. For instance, teachers seek resources and conversation on structural inequities of race, class, gender and sexuality, power, and privilege and how they function in students' access and opportunities in schools. Specific acts of advocacy for our team involved: demonstrating solidarity for students, families, and colleagues who were living intersecting and/or different identities from our own; challenging colleagues' deficit language about students and families; providing transportation to school events or an extracurricular activity; speaking with administrators about policies or public messages at the school that problematically positioned some students and families; or sharing with students and other educators stories of personal experience of racial and other marginalization in school.

Tenet Three: Testimony and Critical Witness to Trauma Are Woven into the Fabric of School Literacies. *These pedagogies, and the affective dimensions of teaching and learning that they inherently encompass, are inseparable from instruction, content, and curricular goals.* Opportunities for testimony and critical witness occur through purposeful use of familiar instructional practices, such as mini-lessons, and the modeled writing, topic choices, multimodal projects, literature choices, and text discussion that occur within them. In addition, moments of reciprocity, vulnerability, and supporting students experiencing trauma occur through the individual interactions throughout the day in classrooms, including the mindful ways teachers locate themselves near students experiencing challenges, a nod, a wink, a gentle hand on a shoulder, as well as the kinds of conversations they take up in individualized instruction, such as reading and writing conferences.

Tenet One: Testimony and Witness Are Reciprocal

In the way I'm using them, testimony and witness are both ideas and actions—and those terms are swirling all around us. From academic texts to novels and TV courtroom dramas, I've noticed that the relationship between testimony and witness is often imagined as linear—testimony is conveyed in some way by one person and it is received by another, a witness. In graduate school I remember eagerly reading Shoshana Felman and Dori Laub's (1992) influential book, *Testimony: Crises of Witnessing in Literature, Psychoanalysis, and History*, which explores how large-scale traumas, such as the Holocaust, are conveyed in literature or film, and what it means to witness those narratives as a reader or viewer. I learned so much from their book, but I remember raising an eyebrow on that page where they describe a witness as "the *blank screen* on which the event comes to be inscribed" (p. 57). It made me think about how life stories circulate in classrooms and how often children have no say in whether and how their lives are shared in schools (I mean, as every teacher knows, those cumulative files are often packed with information!). Viewing the teacher witness as a blank screen or an empty page upon which children's traumas are received and stored struck me then and now as the wrong metaphor. My experience evokes a much more cyclical image of testimony and witness. What happens when you hear someone's difficult experience? There in the empathy, the sympathy (hopefully not simply pity)—isn't there also the inevitable spark of your own story? We know, we live, the ways teaching is a feeling, a sensation, that fills our days (Boldt, Lewis, & Leander, 2015; Leander & Ehret, 2019). Whether you speak it or not (to yourself, even, let alone the person sharing their story at that moment), isn't your experience there? Isn't there some felt connection to the larger themes of another's experience—loss, pain, fear, violence? Witnesses are far from blank screens.

Thinking of testimony and witness in classrooms as a continuous circle brings to mind trauma studies scholar Cathy Caruth's (1996) description of stories of trauma as a "plea by an other who is asking to be seen and heard, this call by which the other commands us to awaken" (p. 9). That awakening she describes speaks to the multiple dimensions involved in witnessing. Imagining testimony and witness as circular positions children as active participators and agents of that process in a way that linearity doesn't. The smooth endlessness of the circle suggests that the compulsion and responsibility to witness and to testify are always present. In this view, the circle of testimony–witness begins when someone's difficult experience enters the classroom (in whatever way that occurs) and demands that others bear witness. Faced with such testimony and in acting as witness, the listener may respond with personal testimony that, in turn, must be witnessed and, again, may prompt testimony from her witnesses.

Yes, when we witness children's lives we must see the child, hear the child. Yes, we must guard against appropriating children's experiences (much more on that caution below!). But we also must be willing and unafraid to awake to our own hard stories. Teachers are not just witnesses to children, but they are also testifiers. We need to let our hearts break in the face of some of the stories our students bring to us and let their hearts also bleed a bit for us. I have learned this from children.

The Importance of Reciprocity. I cannot overstate the importance of reciprocity in pedagogies that support children experiencing trauma in classrooms. In Chapter 1, I touched on some of the reasons why reciprocity is essential and why that idea is woven into the classroom stories throughout the book. It is no surprise, then, that the charge to mindfully invite children to be witnesses to teachers' lives is front and center as a tenet of these approaches. No one gets through life unscathed. Humanity is fragile, in body and soul. Of course, as I discuss further in tenet two below, humans are also horrifyingly adept at creating systems that inflict harm on others. So some bodies are in much more peril than others. Very soon we'll drill deep into the how and why of the importance of seeing the disconnections within connections made with others, and the extremely different and consequential ways individuals can be positioned within stories shared and witnessed. For this tenet, though, let's submerge, cell-deep, into connection.

In short, teachers have to model and engage in the risk and vulnerability of bringing difficult experiences into the public space of classrooms. Sharing the hard stuff of life with others, whether within or out of our control, always makes one vulnerable, always opens one up to the potential for further hurt—and, in classrooms, is a risk that too often falls only on students. For all of those reasons (and more discussed below), teachers must first position students as *their* witnesses. In conversations with children, I have learned to interrupt my initial impulse (that I always failed to act on, mind you) to stay in the role of a silent listener who shouldn't share my own loss or other connected experience. The same applies to teaching, whether in an individual conference, a small group, or whole-class instruction. Children are, without fail, keen and kind in their responses as witnesses.

At the same time that this intentional testimony positions children as witnesses, teachers' sharing serves as invitation and endorsement for drawing on deeply felt life experiences as source and resource for school literacies, including experiences that are hard—hard to experience, hard to share—whether or not it is a story you would attach to the word trauma. Positioning children as our witnesses, with intention, involves some "going there" with ourselves. We have to connect with the stories that get into the marrow of our lives. We have to use our wisdom to shape what we share into what we sense is the age-appropriate choice and form our stories take. We have to set aside our fears and questions about whether our story is "worthy" of children's witnessing. Let's unpack all of those "have to's" in enacting reciprocal vulnerability, because they are not only doable, they will enrich and enliven our teaching and our lives.

Sometimes, in my teaching and research, I encounter a student who is a member of that lost siblings club that I described in Chapter 1, that guild no young person should have to join. When that encounter happens, whether the person is 8 or 20, I'm filled with a pulsating sensation. It's visceral, beyond words, but we could name it connection or recognition. I can't know for sure if it's mutual, but often there is a tumbling of the story, then or soon. At that point, my experience has either been already shared through writing (in the case of university students) or, with children, shared through conversation in those moments of mutual discovery. Similarly, when a child shares an experience related to a family member's incarceration, there is a double-take at my connection. That makes sense. Most of us resonate with those periodic link-moments when someone's wounds seem to be speaking directly to our own. Even when the particulars and consequences are different (and they most certainly always are), when we share a certain kind of trauma with others, we recognize a bond, even if tenuous, even if with very different stakes. The value of those connections is apparent in the collective support systems that many people have formed in relation to shared traumas and struggle—from small circles of chairs in a church basement to the global span of #MeToo. Those shared experiences, even at the broadest level, are so often powerful. You will regularly encounter those kinds of connections as you immerse in these pedagogies.

What Serves as Testimony? By definition, to bring authenticity to positioning students as witnesses, I can only share my own difficult experiences, whatever those may be. Sometimes those experiences are the ones that we *feel* as the pillar challenges of our lives, those that fundamentally shaped the arc of our life's journey or, in a different metaphor, those stories that cut us to the core and get at the center of who we are in the world. Sometimes, however, the stories we share arise from a relatively brief, punctual, experience. It may have us seriously rattled, shaken, maybe literally shaking—that day and perhaps through the week, the month—but is more of a post in our lives than a pillar. The week my infant niece was admitted to the NICU fighting a terrifying bout of pneumonia, I knew I needed to draw on that story in my modeling of a personal narrative writing mini-lesson with the preservice teachers in my course. Two weeks later, our little ray of sunshine was home and healthy, her illness, thankfully, serving as a brief, punctual testimony to my fear.

Now let me be clear, though, about the kinds of experiences that can serve as testimony in your teaching. You don't need to make that determination ahead of time, not at all. You don't need to label or rank your stories of the difficult things in your life. What I wish to convey is just this: A range of stories count and will serve this intentional move in your teaching. You have those stories. We all do. Think about what those are. It may be obvious to you or it may, for some, be far from clear. You'll decide, based on the ages of the children with whom you spend your days, what experiences you can testify to and in what forms. As you make your way through this book, start to consider how you might craft those experiences for sharing with the children in your classroom.

But, you may ask, what if I haven't experienced anything comparable to what some of the children in my class have gone through? I get this question a lot when I write and speak about trauma and literacy. The experiences I share from my own life sometimes fuel those questions from other educators, who, blessedly, haven't lost someone tragically and prematurely, haven't experienced a family member's incarceration, or other life events often marked as "trauma." Some have seen my life experiences as providing direct inroads toward connection with children and don't see how they can paint themselves into that landscape. The question comes from a place of care and being careful. By sharing a story of a challenging time, whatever form that challenge took in *your* life, are you implying that, say, your loneliness after a move away from family and friends is somehow equivalent to a child's loss of an uncle to gun violence? What an important move to question ourselves and guard against imposing our lives on others! But in our classroom inquiries, we saw how running headlong into others' experiences with a visceral rush of resonance doesn't require those stories being the same or even same-ish. It does, though, require meaningful themes that allow various life stories to congregate.

I feel strongly that measuring the "same-ness" of experiences is at cross-purposes with honoring and supporting children experiencing trauma. Why? For one, it implies that we're in a position to characterize and identify what counts as a child's difficult experience. Children, as we'll see, take up invitations to testify to their lives in ways *they* determine. For another, it gives us adults a handy way to opt out of vulnerable pedagogies that usher in aspects of lives that may make some uncomfortable. In other words, it provides a clear path of retreat to safety and the practices, conscious or not, that have marginalized stories of trauma and, thus, the children who have lived those stories. When Megan was concerned that her story wasn't enough, that her experience of her parents' separation or a grandparent's death or the end of a long-term relationship was inadequate in the face of some of the children's experiences of separation—death, premature and sometimes violent, of close family members; incarceration; deportation— she worked through it by leaping in, while reflecting on her feelings and motivations all along the way.

Of course, enacting these approaches can feel risky and spark self-doubt. And those feelings are also connected to the murkiness of boundaries and appropriateness in what and when to share what matters deeply to us.

Those complexities are crucial when seeking to shift our practice toward reciprocity in testimony and witness. In order to open invitations (never requirements!) for children to bring life to literacies, we have to be generous in what counts as the hard stuff we share from our own lives. We have to take whatever we experience in life about which we feel deeply and draw on it—realize it as source of connection and opportunity to practice vulnerability and reciprocity in our teaching. It makes a difference, each and every time I witness it. Lost your dog? Share it—the fear, the dread, the happy or not-so-happy ending to that story. Terrified of rollercoasters, but remembering the supportive grip of your older sister's hand on yours as you pulled that shoulder brace down and pushed on it with all your might to make sure it wouldn't pop open in the middle of the ride? Don't hold that memory to yourself. Tell that story. That story is about the love and support of loved ones in the face of deep fears; the grip of your sister's hand is the detail that illuminates the theme. Connection is in the courage it took for you to pull down that brace. The grip, the courage, the fear—that is what will invite and resonate with others' stories. It's what we do as humans—weave our own stories into the themes of others'. I do believe we can't delay in locating the extraordinary—the risk, fear, dread, courage, loss, connection, absence, hope—in the ordinary routines of our literacy classrooms. Early in the school year, we can do that by exposing our own wounds, whatever those are, in whatever way we know to be appropriate with the children gathered around us. It signals that our lives, children's lives, are the source and resource for literacies. Such moves make space for the power of each moment, each life, including trauma.

So, consider, reflect, decide on a story, choose the context in your classroom (maybe this week) that works to share it, and try it out. Think in the moment and reflect later about how it feels. Does it feel, in your bones, vulnerable? As you speak or write this testimony, is there a sensation you might describe as meaningful—maybe a rush or perhaps more of an ooze? Do you feel invested in how your listeners, your readers, your witnesses, will respond to your experience? If the answer to any of these questions is "yes," it is likely a well-chosen experience to share. If "no," that experience might be an important starting point for you, especially if you are new to considering this kind of intentional move toward vulnerability in your teaching. It is okay to ease your way in. Start planning for the next time and, if it at all feels possible, "go there" a bit more and see how it goes.

The difference is tangible in the classroom. As my collaborators and I moved from intuiting some aspects of these pedagogies to intentionally designing and studying the forms they can take in classrooms, I found myself finding small ways to insert these ideas into my time with children in classrooms where these weren't explicitly part of instruction. For instance, I was in a 3rd-grade classroom at the start of a unit on personal narrative, and the children were brainstorming topics in response to several prompting ideas.

One of those ideas was "Something I lost." The teacher's model was about a lost object, a watch that didn't seem to have sentimental value, and, at the end of the story, finding the watch with a sigh of relief. The children then went to small-group rotations focused on each of the potential topics, where they were asked to write their ideas for narratives on large chart paper. I made a beeline for the topic of something lost. The three children in that group started naming lost objects—a toy, a key, a pencil. I shared, "When I was a teenager, I lost my brother." They raised their eyes from the chart paper to my face, one child said, "Oh, sad." Then, almost without hesitation, the group shifted their brainstorm from objects to people—a grandma's death, an adored cousin who moved out of the house and into his own apartment, a little brother lost in a mall and then joyfully, tearfully found. This was a small moment, but it happens again and again. It is striking to see the parallels between a teacher's model of a topic and what children, for good reason, take up. An opening in the assumption of "what counts" leads to the potential for breadth of possibilities and depth of connections. The lost toy still matters, and may matter a lot, but the lost grandmother is also literally on the page as possibility. Those possibilities allow writers' ideas and connections to proliferate. Those proliferations include invitations to draw on life experiences, including the very hardest stuff of life, as resources for school literacies.

In the coming chapters, we'll encounter several examples of how Megan and other teachers wove their own testimony into their mini-lessons across literacy units of instruction and across the school year in ways that initiated, invited, and sustained a sense of reciprocity in a circle of testimony and witness.

What Is Critical Witness? In the discussion of reciprocal vulnerability and testimony, we purposefully immersed ourselves in the importance and power of compassion, connection, and the sense of being entwined with others that can be fostered when the most deeply felt, affecting, hard stories from lives are shared with intention in classrooms. Enacting reciprocity in sharing difficult experiences positions children as witnesses to teachers' lives, while also signaling a community where those aspects of life are present and included in what it means to engage with school literacies and thrive within them.

Now we turn to the "critical" attached to teachers' acts of witnessing. Given the opportunity, children will be our empathetic, caring witnesses. Surely, those same words speak to what we must bring to our witnessing of children. However, as I've already argued in the preceding pages, as teachers, adding "critical" to our role of witness is crucial. Why? Because the hardships humans live through are interpreted differently and have very different consequences for individuals and groups in the contexts of schools and the wider society.

First things first: How am I using the term "critical" in this context? As opposed to its common and general usage as a negative judgment (e.g., a critical review of a movie) or analytical (as in "critical thinking"), I'm using it in a more specific sense. Following from an area of social theory called critical theory, *critical* here involves critiquing and changing systems, language, and societal structures that work to disempower and oppress some people while sustaining the power and opportunity of others. So, for our purposes, the "critical" infuses witnessing with awareness and analysis of at least three important aspects of children in relation to trauma: 1) how children are variously positioned in deficit narratives of students' and families' lives; 2) the ways that the systems of schooling and the larger society inflict trauma on some children more than others; and 3) the danger of overidentification with others' stories of trauma (even as we must feel deep connection). All of those issues are involved in interrupting the corrosive ways that a focus on trauma can further marginalize some students and families.

Combined with the other two tenets of these pedagogies, reciprocal testimony and critical witness *do*

- position children as witnesses to their teacher's deeply felt life experiences.
- invite children to draw on the fullness of their lives as welcome resource for school literacies.
- allow teachers to identify larger themes for connection and invitation and, in turn, allow children to see their life experiences, including trauma, as part and parcel of what matters in school.

They *do not*

- require or imply equivalences between life experiences that are lived in the classroom.
- in and of themselves assure children's trust or noticeable shifts in response to interactions or activities in the classroom. These approaches are a process, not an event.

Tenet Two: Critical Witness Requires Action and Advocacy

Serving as critical witnesses for students requires pulling others' experiences close, connecting to the shared feelings, fragility, and tenuousness of human experience. At the same time, it requires holding others' stories at a far enough distance to recognize, analyze, and advocate within the very different ways lives are interpreted and impacted by systemic and sustained oppression. Almost by definition, teachers hold some forms of privilege that may differ from some of their students (as professionals who earn a salary and have at least some benefits—even if both are far below what they should be). However, some of us certainly bring more privilege than others into our classrooms. As a White, middle-class, heterosexual, female classroom teacher, I certainly lived layers of advantage entering my first classroom that were not shared by most of the children who occupied that space with me. And I certainly do now, as I still carry those identities into my work with teacher colleagues and children—and have added being a tenured university professor.

Engaging in Critical Analysis. Critical witness, then, involves actively working to engage in critical analyses of the deficit discourses that swirl around discussions of students in so many contexts of education—from frustrated outpourings in the staff room, to analyses of the various "gaps" in achievement, wherewithal, or resiliency presented in those prestigious news outlets or books that gain lots of traction in education ("grit" and "growth mindset," we're looking at you). So embracing a role of critical witness to children means we seek resources and conversation about structural inequities related to race, class, gender and sexuality, power, and privilege and how they function in students' access and opportunities in schools. Some of you live these issues in your very bones. If you are a teacher of color, you don't need to read about how race impacts students' experiences in schools and society in crucial and complex ways. My two daughters don't need to access what it means to navigate the world as a biracial person in the LGBTQ community. They have lived knowledge, and many of you do, too. I have been sexually harassed enough in my life to understand, in my core, the impact of sexism. But I need frameworks and stories that help me analyze the histories and impacts of oppression that affect children, family members, and colleagues whose privilege takes very different forms than my own. Fortunately, the reading and exploring we each determine we need to grow our understandings is engaging, gripping, and stimulating. I've included a list of readings on the book's website (elizabethdutro.com), including fiction and nonfiction, that you can explore to sharpen your own critical awareness in whatever way feels necessary and productive for *you*.

Embracing the critical in our roles as what Winn and Ubiles (2011) wonderfully call "worthy witnesses" also means taking steps to advocate for students and to work toward justice. For instance, teachers in our inquiry team took actions of various kinds, including: speaking up in solidarity for students, families, and colleagues who were explicitly or implicitly the target of marginalizing language or policies; expanding their own knowledge of issues of injustice and some frameworks and language for expressing those understandings; taking concrete actions, such as providing transportation to a school event or an extracurricular activity for a student or guardian facing transportation issues; connecting with students one-on-one when a child was experiencing short-term or ongoing challenges; speaking with administrators about policies or public messages at the school that problematically positioned students and families of color; or sharing with students and other educators stories of personal experience of racism and other marginalizing experiences in school (when it felt personally possible, safe, and powerful to do so).

Serving as a critical witness to children isn't limited to those experiencing trauma, of course. To support all students well, we should always bring a critical analysis to the ways schools are organized, the histories of schooling, and the language about children used in our schools. However, children's navigation of life's challenges, with the turmoil that inherently holds, becomes even more perilous without that critical layer. For one thing, it is a slippery slope between identifying trauma in a child's life and ascribing pathology to children, families, and communities. As one example, one afternoon in the fall of 3rd grade, I hugged Wayne goodbye at the door as usual as the children left for the day. That night, as I learned the next day, Wayne and his mom had to leave their apartment, taking only what they could fit in their old Datsun sedan. In no way was it possible to take Wayne's dog with them. As Wayne explained between sobs when he returned to school 2 days later, a kind neighbor offered to keep Ruffers overnight and take him to the animal shelter in the morning. Wayne and his mom stayed in a shelter for a couple of nights and then stayed with various friends until they were able to get a new apartment several weeks later. Clearly, Wayne's unstable housing situation, as a source of trauma in his life, was rooted in poverty and inadequate social safety nets (and his situation is far from unique). Providing opportunities for Wayne to express his experience in school literacies in whatever way he may or may not choose would be important. I wish I had had pedagogies of testimony and critical witness as an explicit and intentional part of my practice in those early days of my teaching.

However, Wayne's experience also serves as an example of the potential risks of how trauma is approached and why the *critical* in critical witness is so important. If not approached critically, there may be an already-lurking assumption of trauma in Wayne's and his mom's situation—she was young and a single parent, struggling to pay rent and bills on a minimum-wage job, and with no extended family resources to fall back on. It was a situation ripe with potential for judgment or pity or some kind of head-shaking, holier-than-thou combination of the two. Although we should fight for more social safety nets for families, such judgments about Wayne and his mom would be ridiculously unfair and unfounded. Until the rent was raised, she and Wayne were making it just fine. He was absolutely loved and cared for and his needs were met. She was a few years older than I was at the time and was a parent I admired. She brought fun and joy to her child's life in ways I filed away as something to aspire to in my own future of possible parenthood.

Let's linger here on the corrosive power of deficit perspectives in schools. We are awash in credible evidence about how labeling and negative assumptions about some children's lives is a consistent and persistent presence in language and practice in education. We know from decades of research that those assumptions have dire consequences for children's learning and well-being in classrooms. In ways both overt and covert, assumptions that some lives and literacies are "lesser than" others creep into policy, curriculum, and instruction, as well as day-to-day interactions with children and informal chatter among adults. Whatever form those assumptions take, they absolutely marginalize some children and their knowledge (Campano & Ghiso, 2010). Given that racism and economic inequality are so deeply entrenched in the history and policies of the United States (and many other nations), such marginalization is most unconscionably exacted on children of color and those experiencing poverty.

What is the link I'm making here between deficit assumptions and perspectives and considerations of trauma in classrooms? I see that connection as two-pronged. First, because racism, sexism, homophobia, and poverty are the source of so many forms of trauma in our society, it is far too easy for attention to trauma to be wrapped in already existing assumptions of some children's lives as *traumatized*. Second, deficit perspectives are targeted at students of color, those experiencing poverty, and other marginalized identities because there is an (often invisible) assumption baked into the systems of education in the United States that White, economically secure, heterosexual, English-speaking (all of which I apply to myself) ways of being are "normal" and ideal. Thus, from the get-go, human bodies and lives positioned as other than those characteristics face the potential of being viewed as sources of traumas. These truths and consequences of inequitable societies exact their own traumas on children and are part and parcel of considering trauma in our classrooms.

Embracing Complexity in Responses to Trauma. Our mindful critical analyses coexist with the depth of visceral response to a child's trauma. Imagine (and I know many of you are in the midst of this situation as you read this), a child is abused in their home, the evidence is clear, the investigation is complete, and steps have been taken to ensure distance and protection from the abuser. Of course, we, the child's teacher, feel outrage, sadness, fear (is that adult really far enough away?), as we rally our heart to bring its deepest wells of love to that child's school days. With all of those emotions, teachers must also be vigilant about rejecting deficit narratives of children and their circumstances. As Pyscher (2018) writes in her work on students' experiences with domestic violence and implications for literacy classrooms, "knowing how to navigate such intimate connections to violence from birth through childhood culturally resides in the body, mind, and psyche" (p. 59) and is a knowledge that children bring to their navigations of classrooms and adults in positions of authority. This is survival knowledge.

I remember the first time I experienced knowing that a child in my classroom had experienced the unfathomable trauma of physical and emotional abuse. My first classroom was situated in a district in a semi-large city that was feeling the economic impact of de-industrialization. My school served Black, Latinx, and White families in roughly equal numbers and, in my classroom, all but one student's family were facing economic hardship—from no-cushion tenuousness to homelessness. The week after winter break, social services met with the principal, assistant principal, and me to share what had happened to Frankie over the holidays. For good reason, school leaders have to share a child's situation with adults in the school who have contact with the child and family. As Frankie's story became more widely known, I saw for myself, as a brand-new teacher, how some (too many) staff used his trauma against him—and his mother, his neighborhood, an entire economic segment of the city's, state's and country's population, and, in the most barely veiled language, a full category of racial identity and racialized history in the United States. It was in the eye rolls and "Oh, the poor thing, but what do you expect?" over lunch. It was in the sotto-voiced, "Well, you know that wasn't the first boyfriend she'd let live in that apartment with those kids." The pseudo-kindly pat on my just-turned-22 shoulder, "Welcome to working with this population. Get used to it, my dear." I have a body-memory of feeling my own rage toward Frankie's abuser, while also feeling nauseated at the thought of becoming those colleagues: spewing cynical, unfair, racist judgments over paper-bagged lunches. I wish I'd had more explicit tools and language for it, but I now can see my grasping attempts at navigating the rue of necessary emotions and crucial critique in the face of a child's trauma.

Try a thought experiment here. Let's try to imagine the response to an upper-middle-class White child who has been traumatized by an adult. There could be the pitying tone, even some of the judgment, but it is absurd to the point of unimaginable to consider comments that lump together all White people, all wealthy parents, as dysfunctional based on trauma experienced by an individual child. This example is relatively stark (even as it represents a common pattern many of us have noticed over time) and we may each read it and think, "I've heard that too, but that is certainly not me." But, of course, we *all* have to be vigilant to recognize and challenge even the subtlest slip into "us/them" thinking, whether our privilege is Whiteness, economic stability, heterosexuality, speaking the dominant language, being abled in our navigations of the physical world, or other ways we may be positioned differently from children and families in our schools and classrooms. Without the critical in our most full-hearted approaches to children's difficult experiences, trauma can become a context where acidic us/them framing of human lives seeps in.

Will any of us be as vigilant as we wish to be? Speaking for myself, I know with a certainty that I will mess up. Embracing imperfection is necessary to being a critical witness to children's lives. Striving toward the responses and approaches we know we want and need to bring to our teaching means forgiving ourselves when we stumble, when we wish we could grab words just spoken and shove them back in our mouth, when we feel the words we should have said stuck in our throats, long after the school day has ended. Trauma is unsettling and so navigating it in our teaching has to be unsettled. We can't turn this shaky, slippery ground around trauma solid, grippy. Actually, if I run with that metaphor, it occurs to me that if and when the territory of trauma and schooling starts to feel stable, we'd better take that as a wake-up call. In that scenario, someone needs to shake me. Feeling off-kilter, having to make those little adjustments to stay on the beam in the midst of the wobbles—that's what this work means.

Tenet Three: Testimony and Critical Witness Are Woven into the Fabric of School Literacies

In our teacher-inquiry group, we found that opportunities for testimony and critical witness occurred through the purposeful use of familiar instructional practices, including mini-lessons, modeled writing, multimodal projects, literature choices, and text discussion. Each of the upcoming chapters of this book provide specific examples of how this can occur in your literacy instruction, so I won't go into detailed illustrations here. But we can look back at Dimitri's experience at the start of this chapter to see these possibilities in action. When she had that interaction with Dimitri, Megan was at the very start of her intentional use of pedagogies of testimony and critical witness. She had very deliberately chosen the book *Courage* and just as intentionally connected it to her life. She knew that theme would resonate with some of the challenges children were living—from death of loved ones, to illness, to housing insecurity. The vignette about Dimitri also illustrates how witnessing students' lives extends from mini-lessons to individualized instruction such as reading and writing conferences. Those traveling connections in a literacy block allow us to demonstrate personal support *and* invite children to integrate their lives into school literacies. And, as we'll see in the next chapter, interactions with Dimitri and some of his classmates early in the year led Megan to immediately begin doubling down on integrating these pedagogies into her literacy instruction.

The Importance of Individual Interactions. In addition to the specific weaving of testimony and critical witness into instructional routines, there occur throughout the day moments of reciprocity, vulnerability, and supporting students' traumas through the individual interactions in the classroom. Those teaching moves include the mindful ways teachers physically locate themselves near students experiencing challenges, as well as the kinds of conversations they take up in the seams of the school day—transition times, recess or lunch, before or after school. For instance, when we looked closely at video of teachers in our group, we noticed a clear pattern. Teachers were—often unconsciously, they said—literally locating their bodies closest to children and youth who were experiencing challenges (sometimes difficulties caused *by* school). Once we saw the evidence of how those sometimes-subconscious moves mattered in classrooms, we all began to think with intention about those ways we located our bodies in our teaching.

It is also very clear that those planning writing curricula do not always enact this accumulated knowledge about how to build writing communities in classrooms that layer in the support for trauma in an everyday way. I've written elsewhere about how challenges of poverty were dismissed in word and image from the assumptions of a widely adopted published reading curriculum (Dutro, 2010). Other literacy teachers and researchers have also documented how curriculum and classroom practices too often exclude important experiences because they are viewed as "not for school" and are likely to disappear from school altogether (see Gonzalez, Moll, & Amanti, 2005; Johnson & Vasudevan, 2012; Jones, 2004; and Ladson-Billings, 1994, for just a few of many examples). But we *can* find ways to make children's difficult experiences matter.

Here I also want to acknowledge that you may be reading this as someone teaching in a context where you feel almost no wiggle room to innovate mentor texts or even ways of framing and launching lessons. I want you to know that I see you. If that's your situation, our models of compositions of those things that matter most deeply to us can happen amidst other times with students, even when we know we are being closely watched and monitored for sticking to particular scripts and sequences. It might be that we open up spaces to position children as our witnesses during morning meeting or as a pause moment in a read-aloud—moments in the school day that may not be defined as writing time or even the literacy block. And when I'm feeling very hopeful, I consider how the increasing focus on trauma and books like this one and all the good work of so many more can help us advocate with school and district administrators for the crucial importance of innovation in literacy curricula.

ENACTING TESTIMONY AND CRITICAL WITNESS

In Chapter 3 we'll turn centrally to Megan's experience of shifting her teaching toward these pedagogies and the serendipitous experience that provided the catalyst (and brought us into each other's lives). But her experiences and those of other teachers who are making these kinds of intentional moves in the day-to-day routines of their literacy teaching speak to important aspects of enacting these pedagogies. Some of these aspects are practical (When? How often?) and others are principles to help guide and ground us.

Let's start with a couple of important practical questions. When does planned testimony to the difficult happen? How often should you intentionally plan for a lesson that enacts reciprocal testimony and witness? As you've likely gleaned from earlier sections of this book, you can bring these pedagogies to your practice by shifting one text read, one story shared, in a way that positions students as your witnesses and issues an invitation to students. Once the central tenets of testimony and critical witness are absorbed and the commitment is made, these approaches can launch at any point. And right now, a lesson that intentionally enacts these pedagogies can be put in the plans for your current or upcoming literacy lessons.

Certainly planning your own testimony to a difficult experience within a lesson, a read-aloud, or other literacy routine is not something that needs to occur every day or even every week. It needs to be woven into literacy instruction in intentional and strategic ways. If I were to make a very concrete recommendation of how often a teacher's testimony to difficult aspects of life should occur, I would say about once or twice in each unit. If a different measure makes more sense for your context, you might plan for such a lesson or discussion every month or 6 weeks. I can also confidently attest that 1) it *must* happen very early in the year to lay a foundation of reciprocal testimony and witnessing and to proffer an invitation to bring all aspects of life to school literacies; and 2) for that invitation to remain vibrant and present, teachers' enactment of testimony to the difficult must happen *regularly*. However, of course, that must occur in a way that is responsive to children's and teachers' unfolding experiences and relationships, as well as to the curriculum. None of us can predict what might happen to a child next week, to you or a loved one, or to the community (local, national, or global) that will prompt an important and meaningful decision of what will occur in a writing mini-lesson or interactive read-aloud or class meeting conversation. In other words, enacting pedagogies that recognize and honor trauma's presence is neither just spontaneous, nor completely planned in advance. It is both. It has to be, as the pedagogies and the reasons for them are living and breathing in the bodies in each classroom.

Let's turn now to some of the guiding principles to hold close in these pedagogies. First, making intentional space for stories of trauma is always posed as invitation, *never* as requirement. As we'll explore further in Chapter 5, we truly can't know when a child might take up those invitations, so we just keep extending them. For some children, we can trace the subtle ways they move toward expressing their deepest-held trauma across an entire school year. Other children's responses to our invitations may include the powerful way they quietly absorb the realization that this classroom is a space that recognizes that the hard times of life *belong* in school. That realization can make a visible difference in a child's engagement, openness, and sense of being seen and valued—even if the stories or topics written about and shared don't noticeably change.

Second, the shifts in our teaching toward vulnerability and reciprocity are not necessarily extreme, stark changes. For instance, embedding invitations to children as a regular practice in our teaching is as simple (and profound) as shifting the mentor texts we model and select. For most of us, it also doesn't involve having to morph into a different kind of person. Megan, as a key example of this point, was a loving, fun, warm, connected teacher, and highly invested in relationships with children and families. Her students knew about her parents and sister, her partner, her dog. She had pictures on display of people and places she valued. In other words, we can put aside any caricatures of cold, distant teachers in discussions of what we might add to our teaching repertoire to better recognize and humanize children who are experiencing trauma.

Third, though, even within a deep commitment to building relational classroom communities, we may still hold assumptions about stoicism, boundaries, and "appropriate for school" topics. Those are assumptions all of us can productively challenge. Cultural scripts about teaching and teachers, relationships with students, and what aspects of life can enter school are complex and often contradictory. In addition, those tropes are very often based on middle-class, White cultural norms about language, authority, emotions, and what constitutes "normal" and desired ways of being. So, for example, many many movies about teaching and schools feature a (most often) White teacher who becomes the sole source of connection and care for students at her or his school. The students, who are most often students of color and/or face economic hardship, are portrayed as lacking adequate care from their families and communities. A fiercely loving teacher saves the students, each and every time. At the very same time, a persistent "don't smile until Thanksgiving" assumption thrives in teaching, even as any one of us who are teachers have long eschewed any literal acceptance of that motif. Yet, despite knowing that immediate smiles and warmth and enacting those values and beliefs from Day 1 of each school year are crucial, what often persists in our profession is the clinging sense that authority is dependent on boundaries and hierarchies that must be *guarded* and *preserved*. This is the "give an inch, they'll take a mile" mindset that is either explicitly evangelized (I'm looking at you, Doug Lamott, and your problematic promises of championship teaching) or implicitly felt and feared (I mean, we're expected to be "in charge," right?). I'm struck just now by my use of the word "guarded," by which I intended to convey "protected," but that also captures the caution and tentativeness that will not serve us well as teachers seeking to support children experiencing trauma. Similarly, I used "preserved" to mean sustained, but it also evokes pickling, something suspended in a smooth-glassed jar. I want to eat pickles all day long, but I do not want my teaching to be there, sealed and unchanging, on a shelf 10 years from now.

Fourth, we can learn from each and every iteration of our enactment of testimony and critical witness in our classroom. Are all experiences we share bound to have the same impact on any given day, unit we're teaching, or group of children? Surely not—and that is okay. Every story that matters to us deeply holds within it the opportunity to demonstrate vulnerability, to let students serve as witnesses, and to perform with students what will be honored in this, the literacy community you're building together. But of course the stories *you* can share matter. An African American teacher who has felt a rush of fear when the lights of a police car appear in the rearview mirror, and can share that story with students who do or will share that lived reality, deeply matters. Of course that story, shared by a teacher of color, will signal something to children about what they too can share—and what they can know about what their teacher knows in the depth of his or her being. As a White person, my take-up of the topic of racial profiling and risk for people of color at the hands of authorities through mentor texts of others' accounts can never achieve the same impact (though, let's be clear, my use of mentor texts will accomplish much more than silence and avoidance, which must not happen!). And imagine the White child in that teacher's classroom who does not and will not have that specific experience, but *does* have an opportunity to witness others' realities and to connect over the themes of dread, fear, and a very real sense of risk in a punctual moment. Teachers of color, LGBTQ teachers, teachers who grew up working-class or facing poverty all know how important those connections are with children and families (and many have written about it beautifully, too). Being positioned as witnesses to what matters to teachers' lives, what is not easy to recall and recount, makes visible and tangible to children that trauma can be part of the landscape of school, no matter whether or when a child opts to explicitly weave a particular experience into their school literacies (more on that in Chapter 4).

FINDING YOUR PEDAGOGICAL METAPHOR

As I emphasized in the first chapter, one of the richest aspects of these shifts in teaching is how they involve an amalgam of commitments, ways of thinking about the world and how we are all differently positioned within it, tangible instructional moves, and curriculum. I always reach for the best metaphors to describe these pedagogies. I once thought of it as a "tapestry"—a tight weave of all those things listed above. But, no, that didn't work. A tapestry, that amazing weaving of something gorgeous that could not have been achieved or predicted by any single thread, no matter how richly hued, gets us only part of the way there. It points toward crafting something of surprise and beauty from varying materials, each one essential to the resulting creation, and each dependent on the others to get there. Okay, so I do love that metaphor. But pull on one thread or look very closely (with a magnifying glass) and each tiny thread is its own thing. Pull it and it stays one thread. The better metaphor for me makes the ingredients impossible to deconstruct, incapable of detangling from each other. So let's go with your favorite muffin, or the chemistry lab beaker, or the mixing of green, blue, and yellow paint into a shade of teal you can't imagine the world without. That's how these three tenets of testimony and critical witness function together. Let's hold those metaphors close as we proceed. There's no extracting that cinnamon, that dropper of calcium chloride, or that blob of yellow, from what results.

For Reflection, Discussion, and Practice

- Begin to consider a challenging experience from your life that you can intentionally share with your students as part of your literacy instruction. We'll explore how to integrate that sharing into instruction in upcoming chapters, but for now, start thinking about what that experience might be.

- Once you have an experience or two in mind, consider the underlying themes in that experience. Is it loss? Is it fear? Is it distrust? Jot down a brief note for yourself about that story and some possible larger themes connected to that experience.

- If you can, come together with others to share what experiences you're considering and the themes you've identified. What do others see that you might have overlooked?

CHAPTER 3

Pedagogies of Testimony and Critical Witness in Practice

I read Raymond Carver's poem "Lemonade" (2015) for a college class 2 years after burying my brother. Had I been standing when reading it, my knees would have buckled at the too-familiar story of a father's grief after losing his son so viscerally rendered on the page. The specificity of the all-consuming regret: *"if they hadn't shopped the night before at Safeway, and if that bin of yellowy lemons hadn't stood next to where they kept the oranges, apples, grapefruit, and bananas. That's what Jim Sr. had really wanted to buy, some oranges and apples, not lemons for lemonade."* The horrific earworms of self-recrimination: *"[He] still blames himself for sending Jim Jr. back to the car that morning to look for that thermos of lemonade. They didn't need any lemonade that day!"* The relentless desire for a do-over: *"Lord, lord, what was he thinking of, Jim Sr. has said a hundred—no, a thousand-times now . . . If only he hadn't made lemonade in the first place that morning! What could he have been thinking about?"* Carver's words were so close, too close, to home. I knew Carver had long been one of my father's favorite authors, but I hadn't yet read much of Carver's writing. There on the page, in so few lines, was an indelible fragment of the unbearable in an unthinkable loss; the irrational, ceaseless, broken glass thoughts of the grief mosaic. That line that captures the desire for a time-turner—that must surely have been the thoughts spinning through my own father's head that had dropped him to his knees that day in the garden, years later, while I watched unseen from the kitchen window. The poem and its title have forever now become entangled with my family's loss and my frightful, but powerful, adolescent recognition that literature can shift in a heartbeat from a window into others' pain to a mirror of one's own. As you might expect, I felt the presence of Carver's poem as I immersed in Megan's and her 2nd-graders' experiences with the lemon and lemonade unit.

* * *

Could one child have experienced more trauma than Carlton did during 2nd grade? Surely. But the convergence of hard things that had occurred for

Carlton is difficult to absorb. Abuse in his biological family, separation from his parents and siblings through child protective services, foster placements, a move to a seemingly stable foster home but with just one of his four siblings, and, incomprehensibly, a cancer diagnosis just 2 weeks before his first day of 2nd grade in his new school.

Carlton was entering Megan's classroom as she was starting her second year of teaching and just as we were launching our exploration of trauma and literacies. Megan already had goals to dive deep into crafting a classroom where stories of the challenging dimensions of life counted—for connections to school literacies and to others in the classroom and beyond. The goal was in place, but Carlton's experience turned it into an imperative. From the start of his journey through cancer, Carlton's classmates and teacher were there to listen as he described his treatments, watch as he pulled up his shirt to reveal his portacath, ask him questions, share their own connections to his illness, and to spray and wipe their desks each day to keep their room safe for him. Having witnessed his experience—while his full head of dark hair changed to smooth scalp and then to short, bristly new growth—Carlton's classmates' investment was palpable by the time they all joyously celebrated his remission that spring.

In this chapter, I'll dive deeply into the experiences of Megan and her students to explain and explore the presence and impact of pedagogies of testimony and critical witness that consciously attend to those challenging life experiences that enter classrooms. In our inquiry into our design and enactment of these pedagogies, we found that the pedagogies supported all children in bringing what mattered to them to their literacies, while also facilitating support and connection for those experiencing particularly difficult circumstances.

I first met Megan at the end of her first year of teaching. Megan is one of those teachers, then and now, who radiates passion for teaching and children. In our first conversation, she excitedly described her district, school, and classroom. She explained that she was going to loop from 1st to 2nd grade with her current group of students. Megan independently stumbled upon the impact of what we began to intentionally craft as pedagogies of testimony and witness, even as I was beginning to write about such approaches to supporting the visceral, difficult experiences always present in literacy classrooms. I remember the day when our mutual friend Julia, who was Megan's roommate and a doctoral research assistant on my project, launched our weekly research meeting with "I have to tell you what happened to my roommate yesterday. It is so connected to what we're doing!" In a paper for a course in her master's program, Megan wrote about the experience Julia was referencing, a shortened version of which is included here.

> My head was throbbing. I felt feverish. I felt that I could cry at the drop of a hat. It was impossible to even consider making it through

an entire day teaching a classroom of 1st grade students. Yet, the bell rang and my 25 students shuffled into class. Most of the morning was a blur. Eventually, it was time for writers' workshop. I had planned on teaching a lesson on descriptive words, but [when] I gathered the class at the carpet, I explained that because I was not feeling quite myself we were going to do something different in writing than what I had planned. I began to construct a narrative about a note my father had written me before a swim meet in 1996. He wrote, "In the moment you think you can't, you'll discover you can. Always believe in yourself." I explained to my students that during all of the difficult experiences I have had since 1996, I have referred back to my father's words and they have helped me persevere. I continued writing, and explained that I lost someone very dear to me over the weekend. My eyes started to water and despite my discomfort in showing this raw emotion in front of my students, I finished modeling writing my story. My students were still engaged when I finished writing my piece, inquired about my loss and made some connections between my feelings and their own lives. I invited students to share about their difficult experiences in their writing if they felt comfortable. While most of the class got to work, two of my reluctant writers lingered at the carpet. The first student asked me if it would be all right if he wrote about his grandfather [who] had recently committed suicide. Since he lost his grandfather, he told me, he had been lonely, as his grandfather was his best friend. I assured him he could write about his grandfather if he wished to and he got to work immediately. The second student asked to write about the fact that his mother and father are both in prison. Although I had learned of this student's circumstances when I first met with his grandfather, his caretaker, this was the first time he had mentioned the topic. [Both students] worked hard for the duration of writers' workshop, and at the end of the writing time the second student wanted to share his story with the class. As weeks passed, I considered the power of this particular writers' workshop. Although it was unfamiliar being emotional about my personal life in front of my students, I began considering the possibility that my students could be affected by my experiences and, in turn, become more comfortable sharing their own. Perhaps through the sharing of my story they no longer saw me as a flawless, emotionless entity, but rather as a human being.

What Julia recognized in her friend's experience is that Megan had spontaneously enacted and felt the impact of bringing her own testimony to her teaching in a way that positioned her students as witnesses to her life. Megan had a tangible sense that her vulnerability had opened an invitation for children to write about challenging aspects of life that deeply mattered to them. This was the circular, reciprocal process of testimony and witness to lives in classroom communities that I was starting to explore on the page and in my own teaching. Megan enthusiastically and generously invited me to be a presence in her classroom. Soon the half-hour drive between the university and her school became routine, and her students became accustomed to the audio recorders and clicking of fingers over laptop keyboards as we recorded as much of the classroom activities and interactions as we could during our visits to Megan's literacy block each week.

As her second year of teaching began, Megan dove into her commitment to find ways to allow students to be witnesses to important experiences in her life. The two contexts in which she launched this intentional practice were morning meeting and writer's workshop. The second week of the school year, the class sat in a circle on the rug and Megan told the children she wanted to share something that had happened to her the weekend before the school year started. Her beloved grandfather had passed away. And, she told them, since her family lived in a city in a different part of the country, she couldn't be with them, so she felt even sadder and more lonely. Reflecting on that morning, Megan recalled how many of the children "immediately testified to my story by making comments like, 'my grandfather died too,' or 'my aunt died,' or 'I never get to see my family either because they live in Mexico.'" From this point forward, morning meeting became a space where children shared stories from their lives outside of school, including difficult experiences. Both Megan and I were struck by how quickly, as she described, "students started to make connections to one another around various topics, yet another example of testifying to the stories of others."

One morning soon after that morning meeting, Carlton entered the classroom crying uncontrollably. In the hallway he explained to Megan that he had thrown up before school that morning and was feeling really sick. As they filed past Megan and Carlton into the classroom and put their backpacks in their cubbies, the other children shot worried glances at each other. They could tell something was very wrong. Carlton and his foster parents had already told Megan they wanted Carlton to share his illness with classmates whenever he and she felt the time was right. With morning meeting already forming a tradition of sharing and response to important experiences, Megan and Carlton decided the time had come. Megan left her arm draped around Carlton's shoulder as she invited the class to the rug. Children, sensing that this was a particularly significant morning meeting, settled in quietly and soberly. Megan told the children how glad she was that they could be together to talk about something important. "Raise your hand if you've ever been sick," she began. Nearly everyone raised a hand. She explained that Carlton was very sick, that it was not the kind of illness that someone else could catch from him, and that the doctors were trying to help him. "He will get better as soon as he can," she said, "but we can help him by being kind friends." She turned to Carlton. "Do you want to share anything with our friends?" He explained, "I have cancer. It's called Hodgkin's lymphoma." A few of his classmates raised their hands, Carlton acknowledged them in turn, and each shared that they had a family member who had received cancer treatment. Megan explained that Carlton was going to come to school as often as he could, and how they could all work together to keep their classroom especially clean since Carlton had to be careful of germs.

Carlton soon shared more about his cancer experiences during morning meeting. The following week, when announcements were over and it was time to share, he raised his hand and quietly asked if he could show the class his port, an area in his chest where his chemotherapy was administered. Megan told him he was welcome to share it, as long as he felt comfortable. He immediately and eagerly lifted up his shirt and explained, with an air of authority, how the port worked. The other children were full of questions. "Do they put the medicine in with needles?" "Does it hurt?" He responded straightforwardly: "with tubes" and "sometimes." Lily and Ariella then shared about their experiences being in the hospital—Lily had her appendix removed early that past summer and Ariella had a metal plate placed in her leg to repair a fractured bone. As Carlton shared more about his journey through cancer, his classmates often had questions and stories of their own to share around the topic of illness. In addition, children were increasingly sharing other important experiences from their lives—conflicts with peers or siblings, the loss of important people or pets, and economic hardships, such as being evicted or a parent's job loss.

In the next section, I turn to how Megan built on this very-early-in-the-year experience to lay the groundwork for a pedagogy of reciprocal testimony and witness in her writing curriculum. Megan and I were a little awestruck by Carlton's eager sharing of his illness with his peers, as well as the swell of important life stories that entered her classroom. Tracing these stories in those early weeks of that year, we were convinced that the children's desire and willingness to share deeply felt aspects of their lives in school was intimately linked to Megan's, and then Carlton's, testimonies during morning meeting.

INTEGRATING TESTIMONY AND WITNESS INTO LITERACY INSTRUCTION

About 6 weeks into the school year, with literacy routines and structures established within the context of the sense of community and connection that morning meeting had fostered, Megan began to proactively build opportunities for reciprocal testimony and witness into her literacy curriculum. In early October she and the children embarked on a set of connected personal narrative lessons Megan planned as a way to invite children to bring a range of stories from their lives—silly, sad, and scary—into their writing. To launch the first lesson, she told the children, "Authors, we are going to do something a little bit different in writer's workshop today. And I got this idea from a teacher of mine, because I wanted to give you all a chance to talk to each other about different things that have happened in your lives, and tell some stories, and it's also a way for us to keep a collection of stories so if we ever don't know what to write about, we can find something to write about."

Each child was given a sheet of paper that they folded into three equal sections, one for each story of experience. That first lesson focused on pre-writing, with the goal to generate possible topics for their narratives. Megan organized the lesson to include a few rounds of moving among whole-group teacher modeling and discussion, individual drawing and notes around possible topics, and small-group sharing.

Megan intentionally began the lesson with the "sad" stories. For the reasons I discussed in Chapter 2, it matters that teachers start with testimony that feels the most vulnerable. Megan and I had seen the impact of positioning children as trusted witnesses. We wanted the children to have an opportunity to sense an invitation, from the outset, that deeply felt experiences count as a source for school writing.

Megan placed a blank paper on the document camera, explaining, "So the first drawing we're going to do is the saddest. We'll put the happy one in the middle. So on your first box you're going to write 'saddest.' So everyone write that in your first square." The children wrote quietly; many already seemed deep in thought. Megan then told them that she was going to turn off the projector while they all drew their pictures, including her. After several minutes in which the children and Megan quietly drew their pictures, Megan called their attention to the front of the room. She took a few moments to be sure they felt settled and ready to listen, and then shared her picture and the story behind it (which is transcribed here from the audio recording of the lesson).

> My saddest day happened when I was in 3rd grade, and one
> afternoon, it was in July, one afternoon my dad and my mom brought
> my sister and me downstairs to our basement, and said we really need
> to talk to you. And, we didn't really talk like a family like that, so
> it was really strange. And what my mom and dad said was, "Your
> dad is moving out. He's not going to live with us anymore." And
> so, I remember going into my mom and dad's room and I saw some
> suitcases, lots of suitcases, and things where my dad's clothes were,
> and he really was [moving]. He had packed up everything. . . . My

dad moved from our house to the city, where he lived in an apartment. And my dad didn't live with me and my mom and my sister until I was in 6th grade, so for 3 years, he didn't live with us.

As we listened to the recording and transcription of Megan's lesson, we noticed a few moves she makes as she shares this story. In the first part above, she tells the "what" of the story, the events that occurred. In this next segment, she moves to the feelings from the experience, particularly her sense of guilt, and how she has carried those feelings in her life.

And that was my saddest day, because I thought it was my fault, I thought maybe I did something wrong that made him move out and move away. And I didn't understand it—and I still don't understand it, even as a grownup. I don't. I don't really get it.

In the conclusion to her sharing, Megan then moves to positioning the children as highly trusted witnesses to a story from her life that she truly had not shared with many people.

And I haven't really told that to very many people, so if you could be respectful of that and not share that with anyone outside of our classroom, because that's something personal in my life. There are a lot of teachers who don't know that [about me]. So, that was *my* saddest day. Right? Do you all remember your saddest day?

The children nod in response to her question and several glance at their own pictures. Megan paused a moment and then thanked them and smiled, saying, "The next story is your silliest story.

All of the children had listened attentively and somberly as Megan shared her sad story. When they transitioned into their silly experiences and she shared her silly story of a time her dog sat on a freshly made batch of frosted cupcakes, they all laughed together. After their final brainstorming, in which Megan told the scary story of almost getting caught in a thunderstorm on the top of a mountain, the children met in groups of two or three to share the ideas they had generated for their personal narratives. For their sad story topics, children had drawn pictures of lost grandparents, aunts, uncles, and cousins; a father being taken to jail; dogs running away from home; and a cousin deployed to Iraq. For Megan, this lesson's intentional move toward reciprocal testimony and witness in her formal literacy instruction resulted in learning more about her students' lives. She also noticed a surge in children's excitement about their writing. Eager to build on this experience, she quickly followed it with the launch of the "Lemonade Club" personal narrative unit.

THE LEMONADE CLUB UNIT

All of the accumulating experiences with testimony and witness in those early weeks of the school year led to the personal narrative unit Megan designed for later that fall. The unit's name and particular focus, though, was inspired by a mentor text. In light of Carlton's illness, Megan searched for children's literature that might address experiences with cancer. A colleague suggested Patricia Polacco's picture book, *The Lemonade Club*, a story about a student and a teacher who were both diagnosed with cancer during one school year. *The Lemonade Club* begins by introducing two 5th-grade girls, Marilyn and Katie, best friends, and their teacher, Miss Wichelman, who "made their classroom seem almost like home." The metaphors of lemons and lemonade are introduced early in the book through a basket of fresh lemons Miss Wichelman kept in the classroom, which she would point to "almost every day" to remind students that life may include sour experiences, as well as experiences that are sweet like sugar. Life, the book emphasizes, is both and, thus, is like lemonade.

The book is an example, in text, of reciprocal testimony and witness. When Marilyn is diagnosed with cancer, Miss Wichelman creates a context in which the children in her class can serve as active witnesses to their friend's experience. Although Miss Wichelman is certainly portrayed as an extraordinarily kind and attentive teacher, it is not unusual in narratives about classrooms for a teacher to be cast in the role of important witness to the lives of children. However, it is more unusual for stories to show teachers being vulnerable with their students. When Miss Wichelman receives her cancer diagnosis, Polacco shows her gathered with her students, sharing her hard news, and being open about the pain and fear she is feeling.

It is no wonder that *The Lemonade Club* proved an important story for Megan and her students, for it closely paralleled their collective experiences of learning about and supporting Carlton through his illness. As in the story, there was no separating the cultivation of relationships and community in the classroom from the practices of testimony and witness Megan was intentionally pursuing, including the sense of collective witnessing and support for Carlton.

In addition, Megan, like Miss Wichelman, became a consistent visitor at Carlton's home and at the hospital. She forged a close relationship with his foster parents and younger sister. She might stop by with a new book to read aloud to the children. Indeed, Megan first read *The Lemonade Club* to her students during a week when Carlton was too ill to be in school. When she visited Carlton at home that week, she read the book aloud to him and his family. And a few times she stayed with Carlton and his sister for a little while to give the parents a short respite from their intense caretaking. For Megan, this was a tangible challenge to the boundaries between the personal and professional that often exist in schools, but she felt strongly that it was both right and necessary.

At school, Megan followed up the initial reading of *The Lemonade Club* by enthusiastically sharing with the children that their next focus for writer's workshop would be their own Lemonade Club. A few days later, sitting with the children on the rug at the start of their writing, she launched a discussion of the idea, repeated throughout *The Lemonade Club*, that life sometimes gives us lemons, but it also includes lemonade. She explained that each of them would write a personal narrative about a time when life gave them lemons and a time when life was sweet like lemonade. She emphasized that what they chose to write was completely up to them. She then shared a recent lemon experience from her own life that she chose with the goal of opening up a range of what counted as writing topics on difficult life experiences. She told them she had been feeling lonely lately and when she contacted an old friend, hoping to reconnect, she could tell the friend wasn't interested in seeing her. She said her feelings were hurt and it made her feel bad. This story was intentionally different in kind from the experiences she'd shared previously—of loss of her grandfather and her parents' separation—as well as from the many stories of illness and hospitals that had filled the room since Carlton had shared about his cancer. She explained that she would put that experience on her brainstormed list of possible topics for her lemon story.

The children used their writer's notebooks to brainstorm a list of lemon and lemonade topics. Students brainstormed a wide range of topics. From this launching day to the final sharing celebration, The Lemonade Club was the focus of writing instructional time for approximately the next month. For the culmination, the children chose two of their stories, one lemon and one lemonade, to take through the writing process and publish in a class book. The class also held a culminating event, attended by some of the school staff and family members, where each child could read aloud whichever story they wished. Importantly, children knew they could share their stories in any language they chose and, if they felt strongly that they didn't want to include their narrative or be the one to share their story, they also had the option of not sharing or of having a peer or Megan read their story.

In this next section, I include a small sampling of the stories children wrote for The Lemonade Club unit, sharing lemon narratives that represent themes present in the stories across the children's writing. For each child, I share both their lemon and their lemonade story, as the relationship between the lemon and lemonade stories was striking and important, particularly for some children. Taken together, the lemons and the sweet stories the children wrote testify to the lemonade-ness of life, the interweaving of the new puppies and birthday parties and the disappointments and unspeakable losses in life. We need our commitments to centering trauma as powerful pedagogy to nest in the knowledge that all of us, children and adults, experience joys along with pain, silliness along with sadness.

CHILDREN'S STORIES

Let's begin with Dimitri, who, a month earlier, had sat paralyzed by what seemed to be the realization that the only topic he was compelled to write about was the very topic he felt was not okay to bring to school. During the lemonade club unit, he chose to write about his grandfather's suicide in more detail.

Dimitri's Lemon, by Dimitri

Someone slammed the door. I went to my mom's room. My mom said, "Come sit down. Grandpa died. He shot himself in the head three times and they took him to the hospital but he died." I cried. I felt lonely because he was the only one in the house who paid attention to me. When I was done crying, I sat on the couch and then my cousin gave me a toy. The toy made me feel a little bit better.

Dimitri and several of his classmates centered their lemon stories on the deaths of loved ones. They portrayed the pain of loss, capturing vivid memories of their loved ones and how they lost them. Dimitri, in just a few lines, painted a portrait of his relationship with his grandfather and the devastation of losing the person in his life who "paid attention to me."

His lemonade story was full of joy and connection—and held echoes of his lemon story.

Today's Lemonade

Ding! Ding! The bell rang. I ran to my mom. My mom drove the car to the mall. I went into the mall and went to the pet store. I saw a rabbit, a spider, and a yellow lab. My mom thought she would pick a black puppy, but instead she picked a yellow lab. Then, we went home and took her for a walk. We named her Sandy. I am happy that Sandy is my dog. I love her to death!

Dimitri's lemonade story brought to full bloom a seed that was present in his lemon story: that life brings comforts amidst grief. Whereas his lemon story captured how an object, a toy given by his cousin, provided a glimmer of solace in the depths of sadness and confusion, his lemonade story centers on a source of joy and connection often unparalleled in many a childhood memory bank. There is no extracting this recent experience with warm, wiggly puppy love from the loss Dimitri is also grieving in 2nd grade.

Although many children wrote about loss, it came in different forms, including systems that separated children from family members. Like other children over time in Megan's classroom, Lorenzo wrote about an incarcerated parent, including these excerpts from his longer story:

Dad Going to Jail, by Lorenzo
My lemon is about my dad going to prison. My dad said that he was going to go to my uncle's house with his friends to visit. He didn't come home that night . . . so we knew his friends were lying and my dad was in prison.

When we went to go visit my dad I started to cry because I was really sad for him. I got to talk to him between a glass. I said, "I hope you get out soon." When my dad got out, he only got to stay with us for a week because he got in trouble again. After my dad left again, I said to myself, "I don't want to go to prison because it isn't a good place to be." When my dad gets out this time, I hope he doesn't go there again.

Lorenzo follows the entering, exiting, visiting, entering again, a story connected to systemic injustices within the United States' legacy of discriminatory economic, political, and social practices that include disproportionately high arrest and recidivism rates of people of color (Reisig, Bales, Hay, & Wang, 2007; Stoudt, Fine, & Fox, 2011). Near the end of his narrative, his thoughts shift toward fear about the future, concluding with a feeling of potential threat for himself, telling himself he does not want to go to prison. Prison, and his understandings of that institution, represent a threat to his father and also an imagined future Lorenzo fears and vows to avoid for himself.

His lemonade story centered on a family gathering at his grandmother's house that features his dad as a central character.

My mom went in the hot tub, but my dad works at 4:30. It was 4:00, so my dad had to hurry up and my dad works far away. My dad is a security guard at [a grocery store]. Every day he brings me a surprise, and my brother, when my dad gets home.

His account showed his keen awareness of the details of his dad's life, including his work and schedule. He highlighted a special parent-children tradition his father had established, underscoring the loss and frustration present in his lemon story.

Lara also wrote about separation from loved ones, recounting the day her uncle was arrested in an ICE raid at his workplace, his subsequent deportation, and the impact on her family.

The Sad Story, by Lara

I need to tell you something. I heard my uncle say something to my dad. I thought that it was going to be something good but it was not so good news. He said I'm going to work the whole weekend in a far place. Then on Monday afternoon he went with his whole company to eat. They were waiting for the food. Then the police came *wiow wiow*. The policeman got out of his car and said: "Identification!" But my uncle didn't have any, so he and four people had to go to jail! But then the police left him in Mexico. Now my aunty is leaving to Mexico because my uncle is in Mexico. It is not the same thing without them because they always used to come and visit us and, when it was Christmas, he would bring lots of presents and he would say to do some tamales and we would make some different food called bunuelos! The End.

Lara's story captures moments of loss marked by confusion and fear imposed by immigration policies. She recreates the chaos and alarm of a routine work lunch shattered by law enforcement whose unexpected, forceful presence holds dreaded and dire consequences for her uncle and his co-workers. Her writing also portrays the intricacies and intimacies of her family relationships—the love and support are palpable on the page, as are the holes left by the absence of her uncle and aunt.

Like the other children, Lara's lemonade story, focused on friendships, holds glimmers of resonance with her lemon narrative.

My Friends!

One day the sky was as blue as a light crayon. When I started 1st grade I met some friends, but I already knew one of them named Melissa. I just needed to meet Dani, Roslyn, and Gabriela. Then we started to get used to each other, then got to play with each other, and we started to ask questions like, "What do you do at your house?" And, when we were away from each other, we would say what happened to us and why it happened. Then we would feel better from telling us. We always started to feel happy and better. Then we would laugh together.
The End

Lara captures how trusted friends are solace in the hard times, holders of one another's experiences, and a path toward feeling better amidst what life brings.

Javier's stories reflect the intimate relationship between the difficult and the celebratory. In his lemon story, he wrote:

Vroom Vroom we were going back home. When we got there I looked over at my Dad. I knew that my Dad was sick. My Dad said he will be in the hospital for ten days. I said why are you going in the hospital. For I can be good and to check my tummy. When the ten days were finished me and my family went to see my dad in the hospital. The nurse said you can go back with your family, but you can't ever do drugs anymore.

His lemonade story was also about his father's challenges with drug use.

When my Dad wasn't sick anymore I said *yaa-hoo* because my Dad can take us anywhere we want. We were at the freemarket. I heard some popping popcorn. We got some. But when I saw my dad doing drugs, I said don't smoke anymore Dad because you'll make me cough. So he smushed it and threw it in the trash. We went to get some water and toys. We went to Walmart. We bought some chicken. We went back home. We had a tradition.

Javier's special day with his dad reads as a chapter two to his lemon story. His father, out of the hospital, is not heeding the nurse's instructions. He listens to Javier, though, and, with the drugs "smushed," they have their special day, a day that marks a new father-son tradition.

The children convey a child's-eye view of these experiences, at times capturing partial understandings, but always including poignant and descriptive details as well as often startling and compelling insights. Without explicit attention to creating space for the difficult to enter and serve as valued material from which to explicitly draw in supported ways in school, it is not just the "lemons" from some children's experiences that would no longer count in school, but also the stories they chose to illustrate the lemonade of their lives. In their experiences and for many children, the sour and the sweet are dissolved into one substance. If their traumas are not invited, children will correctly sense that what school wishes to hear is the mundane and the safe, and they will leave silent what matters most.

REFLECTIONS ON THE LEMONADE CLUB UNIT

As would be the case in any group of more than 20 people, the children had experienced, and chose to write about, various kinds of challenges they had faced, from those I discuss above to the struggle to learn to tie shoes or feeling bad about a fight with a friend. What the Lemonade Club unit offered was a context in which all experiences were officially endorsed and honored. It also was a space in which Megan experienced the impact of this shift in her practice to intentionally build reciprocity in testimony and witnessing into her literacy instruction. The children's writing speaks to the possibilities of pedagogies that tangibly attempt to show that the sharing of hard stories is a risk that can be taken and, if one chooses to put those stories on the page or talk about them while sitting in a circle on the rug, would not be taken alone.

The children's and Megan's experiences that I've shared in this chapter serve as an example of how testimony and witness can weave into and grow within the instructional contexts and daily routines of the literacy classroom. But what does that look like across the genres taught in elementary classrooms, especially in the midst of addressing standards and state assessments? How does a teacher draw on these pedagogies across a school year, and how do children respond? The next two chapters take up those questions.

FOR REFLECTION, DISCUSSION, AND PRACTICE

- Imagine a literacy unit you could craft or adapt that centrally and mindfully takes up pedagogies of testimony and witness, while also achieving the instructional goals you need to address. Try to move away from a feeling of pressure and toward a dream-space of what would be engaging and powerful for you and your students.

Consider:

  » What literature might you choose as focal and/or mentor text(s)?

  » What testimony might you share with students (as modeled writing, as response and connection to a text)?

  » Imagine enacting this unit in your current classroom (or last year's class, if you're reading this in summer). What life experiences do you imagine children might bring to their literacies?

CHAPTER 4

Testimony and Critical Witness to Trauma Across Genres

I remember holding the brand-new journal in my hand. I don't know which family acquaintance handed it to me in those initial fuzzy days amidst the steady stream of faces, food, and flowers. But I do know that the blue and purple paisley-covered journal was the perfect object at the perfect moment. Opening it, I felt then, as I still do now, the potential of blank pages. I had been a writer from my first encounter with a pencil, feeling comfort and more myself using words spilling from my fingers than through my vocal chords. But that gifted journal beckoned like none before. Did someone suggest that I write my entries as letters to him, or did I come to that on my own? However and whoever, I wrote my first letter to my little brother in that very first week of uncomprehending absence. I continued to write, not every day, but often enough, until it was filled up and I rushed to buy its successor.

Contemplating genre in testimony to trauma took me back to my own journeys through genres. I thought of that paisley journal and its epistolary form. Those letters were a source of connection to Kenny, my most trusted secret-keeper. As memories lost their sharpness, those letters remained my clearest window into my grief-consumed adolescence. I thought of the poem I wrote in those first weeks about my brother and what it meant to lose him. It was several stanzas, all rhyming couplets. I had it printed on substantial, ivory-hued paper, at a print shop in town (no home laser printers for DIY fancy print jobs), and I remember the kindness in the shopkeeper's gaze, the sympathy in her voice when I went to pick up my poem. I framed it and gave it to my parents on Kenny's would-have-been 14th birthday that first August. I thought of when my journaling shifted from letters to narrative accounts of my life—no fanfare, no decision, just a transition. And I thought of how, as the years unfolded, my research and the expository genres it takes was and is fueled by my encounters with loss, in explicit and implicit ways. As I wrote, I was also consuming novels, short stories, memoirs, poetry, films, television shows, picture books, essays, research articles, and book-length scholarship. How had I not paused before to consider the head-spinning proliferation of genres that had propelled me into connection with and through the biggest themes of my life?

*   *   *

Tracing the difficult in children's literacies is a light-tripping journey across a year in a literacy classroom. Indeed, dwelling in a child's writing that testifies to the hard stuff raises important questions about the contexts and genres in which children might pursue connections between difficult life experiences and school literacies. In previous chapters we've discussed the reasons why teachers might commit to invite those connections with careful intention. And Chapter 3 focused on a portrait of a full unit on personal narrative and how children responded to an instructional invitation to bring the challenging experiences of their lives to their writing. We also delved into how some children's stories of trauma were inextricable from their stories of joy. Children's writing illustrates how loss, love, longing, belonging, fear, and comfort are, so often, wrapped up in one another as lives unfold.

In this chapter, I'll turn to when those explicit invitations to weave trauma into school literacies might occur, how often, and the forms testimony and critical witness can take across a school year. To take up those questions, we'll turn to genre, that ever-presence in literacy curricula and common way of organizing literacy instruction across a school year. We'll turn to specific examples of what it looks like to enact pedagogies of testimony and critical witness in the varying genres taught in elementary classrooms. The examples I share focus on writing, but we can imagine how the hearts of these examples also speak to responses to text and making meaning with text that may be taught in other parts of your literacy instruction.

Since Chapter 3 was focused on personal narrative, I'll start with other genres typically included in elementary literacy curricula and end with further exploration of personal narrative. As we explore each genre, you'll see how the shape of children's responses varies in the forms that life's complexities and longings take in school literacies. What remains consistent, though, is the remarkable and powerful way children weave their deeply felt, difficult experiences into their school literacies—with all the knowledge and insight those experiences hold.

That power is certainly in Lara's "lemon" story from the last chapter, which includes this image I will never shake, nor would I ever wish to: her uncle smiling at the door at Christmas, his arms full of gifts, his voice ringing out, "Let's do the tamales!" It's the uncle who had just been deported to Mexico, the chaos and confusion of the raid at his workplace also brought to sharp relief in Lara's story. Absence, loss, inhumane and violent immigration policies, and the cascading consequences of distant adults' control over children's lives—it's all there in the piercing "woo woo" of the sirens, the smell and taste of those tamales, and the now-emptiness of that Christmas doorway.

GENRE STUDY AND TESTIMONY TO TRAUMA

In my teaching and research, I bring a central hope related to school writing, one that I know is shared widely by literacy teachers. I wish for all children and teachers to be caught up in a collective feeling that each young author's writing *matters*, that each member of the community has something important to say, and that those ideas can be expressed, valued, and honored. That is the felt sense of writing and being a writer that can transcend genre, infusing all writing with the potential to be grounded in what matters most and a source of conveying a writer's voice and knowledge. Certainly some genres we teach are more or less conducive to explicit and personal expression of the difficult experiences of our lives. That is the key reason why I wish that personal narrative could be the launch unit for each school year at every grade level. Writing stories from the "I" position lays a path to building a classroom community grounded in testimony and critical witness.

However, the genres that *seem* less connected to the deeper dimensions of our lives can be intimately connected to what we've gone through and what we feel most intently. The sense of connection to and through writing that we build in our classrooms travels across genres. We know from many studies of writing and communities of writers that a felt investment in writing is crucial to children's opportunities to grow as writers (Bomer, 2010; Souto-Manning & Martell, 2016; Vasquez, 2016). As teachers, we recognize investment when we experience it with students—it is a source of electricity for our teaching souls. Invested writing, reading, and researching matters for all students, but it is a central route to supporting children experiencing trauma in each and every genre we teach.

In the illustrations in this chapter, we'll encounter a range of ways that these pedagogies were taken up in Megan's classroom across 3 years, as well as in my own and some other teacher collaborators' classrooms. Along the way I will situate these particular instructional experiences in the context of the larger unit in which they're embedded. Also, in each genre example in this chapter, we'll see how teachers attend to curricular goals and standards as part and parcel of taking up pedagogies of testimony and critical witness. I organize this chapter by poetry, letter-writing, informational/expository (research reports and persuasive/opinion), and narrative (including personal narrative and fiction) genres.

The classroom examples in each section serve two purposes. First, each section will show how a teacher took up invitations to testify to trauma in a particular genre, so you can see what it looked like and how children responded. Second, each example is also an illustration of a pedagogy of testimony and critical witness that is helpful *across* genres as you craft your approach in your classroom in ways that serve your students, your teaching context, and who you are in your life and your teaching. In other words, something may spark for you in the poetry example that pulls you to choose a particular mentor text in your persuasive writing unit.

POETRY

Poetry is not only dream and vision; it is the skeleton architecture of our lives. It lays the foundations for a future of change, a bridge across our fears of what has never been before.

—Audre Lorde

Reading through my collection of quotes about poetry, I'm struck that the quotes themselves *are* poetry. It's clear in Lorde's words for poetry: dream, vision, foundation, bridge across fears, skeleton architecture of life. In approaching poetry with children, I wish for nothing more than to convey those powerful and magical dimensions of the genre and what it offers. "Skeleton architecture" so evocatively points to why poetry is a genre that beckons expressions of trauma. The flesh on those skeletons is brought by the poet. When children are offered encounters with poets (their teacher, as well as published poets or other mentors) who fill the frames of language and form with the heart, muscle, tissue, and bone of struggle, loss, fear, longing, they so often seize this genre. And, also often, they pursue their poetry in breathtaking ways.

Below I provide an extended example of poetry as part of a literacy lesson, followed by examples of how children responded to that particular lesson and the form of poetry it included. I then share some of the poetry children wrote across the 3 years of our inquiry in Megan's classroom. The children's poems illustrate the various ways children responded to the invitations offered to bring trauma to their poems in a context in which testimony and critical witness were woven into their literacy instruction across the school year.

In the book *Because of Winn-Dixie* by Kate DiCamillo, 10-year-old Opal's mother's absence looms large. Opal's mother abandoned her when Opal was 3 years old. The short novel tells the story of Opal and her father's move to a new town. Soon after they arrive, a stray dog appears at their home and quickly becomes a central point of connection and comfort for Opal. She names the dog Winn-Dixie after the grocery store in her new southern town. Many of you know this book, I'm sure, and can recall the masterful way that Kate DiCamillo conveys how children's bodies can hold multitudes—loss, love, memory, immediacy, absurdity, silliness, solidity, chaos, connection, confusion, and deep wells of wisdom—as they inhabit the day-to-day of lives that are, by definition, not entirely of their own making.

In the winter of the first year of our inquiry in her classroom, Megan chose *Because of Winn-Dixie* as a read-aloud, knowing that it would also serve as a powerful mentor text for the poetry unit that she would be teaching in writing. Given the book's themes, she knew it would provide connections to children's lives, as well as a context for sharing her own testimony and positioning children as her witnesses.

I arrived in the classroom for writer's workshop the day Megan planned to draw on the book for her poetry writing mini-lesson. The children were gathered in their usual spot for the writing workshop mini-lesson, sitting cross-legged on the rug as Megan sat in her purple-painted chair facing them, with a blank page of large chart paper on an easel to her right. She held *Because of Winn-Dixie* in her hands as she launched the lesson.

Megan: "Who can tell Ms. Elizabeth what happened yesterday when I was reading *Because of Winn-Dixie*? So, we're reading *Because of Winn-Dixie*, and I want to know if someone can tell her what happened. Let's see, umm, Larry."

Larry: "So, he got lost."

Megan nodded, "So, he got lost—and that was what we read. But something happened to me as I was reading a part of the book. What happened? Carlton?"

Carlton looked up at Megan, "You started to cry because, um, because, I forgot what your dog's name is, but you, you lost him."

Megan nodded, "Jonah. Well I didn't lose him, but I had to give him up." Several children responded with, "Why?"

Megan paused briefly, then explained, "Well, I had him with a friend of mine, and Jonah was my birthday present, and then my friend and I stopped being friends. And when we stopped being friends, he took the dog."

"How come?" a child asked, "when he was yours?"

"Because he wasn't a very good friend." She paused briefly, then continued, "But, I was reading this part of *Because of Winn-Dixie*, and it inspired me to write a poem. So I want to reread [that part of the book] because it really . . ." Her voice trailed off. "And then I'll tell you all the rest of the story. But let's remember. Winn-Dixie ran away and Opal was thinking of ten things that she remembered about Winn-Dixie."

Megan reread a passage describing what Opal is thinking about as she and her father search for the dog:

Ten things she remembered about Winn-Dixie like ten things that she remembered about her mom, and here they were. . . . Number one was that he had a pathological fear of thunderstorms. Number two was that he liked to smile using all his teeth. Number three was he could run fast.

Megan looked up from the book, "And so last night, when I got home, I was thinking. I had been thinking all day about how that made me get a little bit emotional. And I got home last night and I said, you know what? I think I'm going to call. I don't want to talk to [my former friend], but I want to leave a message for Jonah. For my dog, Jonah. So I called and I said. 'This is Megan. This message is actually for Jonah.' And I said, 'I am calling to wish Jonah a very happy fourth birthday, and I want him to know that his momma misses him so much, and thinks about him all the time, and will you please give him a big hug and kiss for me on his birthday. Okay, bye.' And I was really happy that I did that, because I do miss my dog very much."

When I looked back at my notes from that day, I noticed my use of words such as "riveted," "hushed," "rapt," and "eyes locked on their teacher" to describe the children as they listened and responded to Megan's sharing.

She continued, "So, I was thinking that today what I would write for you is a poem about my dog Jonah. And sometimes what people do when they write poems, is they make their poetry sound like another author, or another poet. So I'm going to kind of copy Opal and I'm going to write ten things about my dog, Jonah."

Megan turned to the chart paper and picked up a marker. "Number one is Jonah loved to swim. He was the best swimmer at the dog park. Number two. Jonah liked to sleep on my bed. His hair was everywhere, and he felt like a little heater." Here she shifted from thinking aloud about the content of her poem to voicing future revisions: "I'm going to have to change some of these words, cause I'm using 'liked' and 'loved' a lot, and I remember those are kind of boring words, so I'm going to go back and change them. Number five," she paused, "What else can I tell you about my dog Jonah?"

At this point in the interaction, children began to chime in spontaneously with ideas and questions as Megan continued to draft her poem in front of them. "Ms. Henning, wouldn't that be funny if Jonah went mountain climbing with you?" one child asked with a smile. "He did! He has!" she responded. "Like, climbing the big rocks!" another child exclaimed. "Yeah! Haven't I ever showed you that picture of us?" A couple of students said, "No", while others nod. The children began to ask what Jonah looked like while Megan walked to her corner table to pull her writer's notebook off a shelf. Leafing through the notebook as she returned to the rug area, she exclaimed and held a page open for the children to see, "Here's my dog, Jonah. Right there. Do you see him with his face under the bed?" The children oohed and awwed over pictures of her dog. She then turned back to the "10 Things" poem she was drafting and let out a little laugh. "Listen to this one! This is kind of like what we were talking about yesterday in science." "Jonah had extremely bad gas" she wrote as her next line.

Carlton: "Was it smelly?"

Megan: "It was *very* smelly."

Carlton: "Ewww"

Megan: "I like that word Carlton. I'm going to use that—smelly—instead of bad. It means he farted a lot."

Carlton and other children laughed and others wrinkled their noses. Megan continued to talk aloud and children chimed in with questions or comments as she wrote. After the last line of the poem, Megan said, "So, those are ten things that I remember about my dog Jonah."

This vignette from the classroom illustrates some principles about enacting testimony and witness in a poetry-writing lesson that speak to multiple layers of taking up these pedagogies. I hope this example looks quite straightforward to you, because that's the intent. For many of you, this doesn't feel like upending your current practice. However, it may very well, for most of us, represent some significant shifts we can take up that will open up school literacies to the traumas children may be experiencing.

For one, Megan used *Because of Winn-Dixie* as the mentor text for a poetry lesson with planning and intention. The text's themes connected to challenges children were facing in her classroom, including absence and loss of parents and other family members. It was a novel that could travel across contexts of literacy—read-aloud and writing mentor text being just two of the many we might imagine. For another, the interaction also shows the presence of joy, laughter, and irreverence as part of these pedagogies. In addition, this example reveals how a teacher can draw on an experience that, though challenging, is not comparable to some of the other traumas in the room. Yet children empathize and, as we'll see, they make their own connections and decisions about how they might take up these themes or forms in their poetry.

When Megan completed the draft of her poem, she turned her attention to the instructional goals for the mini-lesson, which that day focused on what writers consider when revising their poems. "What did you notice that I did as a poet? What did I do?" she asked the children. "Turn to your partner. What did I do today?" After the turn and talk, children shared ideas, including: You put your feelings into your writing about Jonah; you included details of things you remember about him; you changed more boring words to more interesting words; and you got ideas from a book you had a connection to. The class discussed each idea, with Megan using her marker to point out what each child was noticing about her draft. She recorded their ideas as a list on another page of chart paper so children could refer back to it as they worked on their own drafted poems. They then discussed goals they would pursue during independent writing, including working on an illustration for the poem they had chosen to publish in their class collection of printed poems and an invitation to write their own 10 Things poems when they'd finished their picture. Megan reminded children she would be conferencing with some of them about the poem they were publishing.

Some of the children responded to Megan's lesson and their experience with *Because of Winn-Dixie* by constructing their own "10 Things About . . ." poems. A few children wrote about their own pets, sometimes a pet that had died or was lost in other ways and sometimes a pet still thriving at home. For example, Reyna wrote a "10 Things" poem about the dog she had loved that no longer lived with her, which started: "#1 Hersey extremely loved to fetch, #2 He ate people food, not dog food, #3 He bit my dad a lot." Each of her ten lines conveyed another detail.

A few children took the themes of loss, fear, confusion, and frustration from the book and Megan's connections, and used the 10 Things form to write about people in their lives. For instance, Javier wrote,

1. He is in jail.
2. He used to drink.
3. He used to fix things.
4. He used to do dad things.
5. He got stabbed.
6. He used to have a fast car.
7. He always go into a fight with my mom.
8. My Dad ran from the cops
9. He had a bunch of bad friends.
10. He had to live with my Grampa.

Javier's poem conveys the complex mix of memories infused with both wistful regret and straightforward recounting of his father's actions and circumstances that would have been fraught, frightening, and painful for Javier to witness. Like the poem the protagonist writes in *Because of Winn-Dixie*, the poignancy of the loss at the center of Javier's poem is punctuated by the list form it takes.

Across the 3 years of our inquiry in Megan's classroom, children consistently brought challenging experiences to their poetry. It was winter of that 3rd year when Sonia wrote her poem, "All My Brothers." Sonia had experienced the kinds of multiple traumas that accumulate in too many children's lives. She was in kindergarten when child protective services stepped in to remove her and her four brothers from their home. I wasn't privy to the details—just understood the children had experienced abuse and neglect. One of her brothers was Carlton, who had entered Megan's 2nd grade two years earlier, close on the heels of his cancer diagnosis (and who I introduced in Chapter 3). Sonia and Carlton were kept together in the same foster home, but their three older brothers were sent to other places. It was never quite clear to me where they were, but what was crystal-clear was how much their two little siblings grieved their absence. The periodic sibling visits would appear in both Sonia's and Carlton's writing in variations of "not enough." During the poetry unit, Sonia wrote a poem about each of her brothers and gathered them as stanzas in one longer poem.

All My Brothers

Jay
Red hair, my brother has red, long hair
I love my brother Jay.
Jay is very kind.
I barely get to see him.
I wish I could see him every day like I get to see Carlton.
I love him a lot.

Randy
Randy is very kind.
I love all my brothers, but I really love him.

Carlton
Carlton has cancer.
He could have died.
I am very happy that he did not die because
If he died I wouldn't have a brother to live with.

Luke
Luke is very nice.
I love him.
He is kind.
I barely get to see him.
I love him.

Sonia's poem serves as beautiful tribute to her brothers, as well as expression of her longing for the daily connection she has lost. In her stanza about Carlton, she also captures the weight of fear, knowing the brother she still has with her could have been taken from her with such unfathomable finality. The other stanzas have parallels in structure and meaning—her love for her very nice, very kind brothers, her missing of them—but Carlton's is wholly focused on the threat of his death and the loneliness and isolation that would have followed.

   Children expressed various feelings related to difficult events or to loss in their poetry. Sometimes it is anger and frustration, as Lily captured in her poem below about her mother having to find a different home for her dog. Notice how she ensures her readers are invited first to understand the bond between pet and child, how she uses present tense to describe her dog (I *have* a dog), and then shifts readers to her anger and sense of injustice in the final stanza, underscoring the sense of what is lost.

> **My Dog Angel**
> I have a dog
> She is big
> I love her
> She is awesome
> I love her best.
> I will call my dog
> She comes to me.
>
> **I am so mad**
> **Because my mon**
> **Gave away my dog**
> **I am mad.**
> My mom gave it to my step mom.
> She gave it to my grandma.
> (Bold text is in original)

It won't be a surprise to most elementary teachers that pets are a persistent topic in children's writing, including their poetry. Megan's classroom was full of pet poetry each year, especially following her modeled poem about the dog she had lost. Teachers attuned to the intricately connected veins of children's lives will also recognize that pets are in no way distant from trauma for many children. For sure, the death or other loss of a pet can be a source of grief in itself for any child. However, as we also saw in the Lemonade Club unit in Chapter 3, for children facing particular life challenges at any given time, the role and presence of pets can take on extra layers of significance—sources of comfort, fun, and stability. And sometimes loss of pets is connected to families' struggles with poverty or other inequities.

We should rightfully worry if we sense a shrinking presence of poetry in elementary literacy curricula. Some educators have suggested this could happen as the increased focus on informational text is now established through the Common Core Curriculum Standards and the state standards that closely model them (Maranto, 2015). However, poetry is decidedly not absent in those standards and, I hope, is still part of your literacy teaching experience each year.

LETTERS

To send a letter is a good way to go somewhere without moving anything but your heart.

—Phyllis Theroux

In the second year of our study in her classroom, Megan launched a short writing unit on letter-writing. The curricular goals for the unit focused primarily on purpose and form, so children would have the genre in their repertoire. Although a shorter unit than the other genres, Megan and I were struck by how many children harnessed it in meaningful and moving ways, demonstrating the power of the genre in ways we couldn't have anticipated. I have little doubt about what set the stage for the children's take-up: Megan made a key decision about how to launch the unit that expanded the possibilities of who a letter could be addressed to.

As children sat on the rug where the class always gathered for writing mini-lessons, Megan turned a page on the large chart paper on her easel. She revealed a letter she had written and explained that they were going to think together about letters—why we write them and what they include. She explained: "When I thought about writing a letter that I could share with all of you to start our new writing unit, I thought about how I wanted to write to someone very special in my life. And I thought about how letters don't have to be written to people who we get to see in our lives, though they can be. Letters can also be a way to connect to people who we don't get to see and who we miss. So I decided to write to my grandpa, who died a few years ago. He was very close to me, very special. This was my Dad's dad. I called him Papa." She then read her letter aloud.

Dear Papa,
 I miss you. My dad misses you. We talk about you all the time. Sometimes we remember the silly things. Like when your hair would stick straight up in the morning or when you would pull your pants up high above your belly button. Sometimes, we listen to the music played at your funeral, "Fanfare for the Common Man," and we cry together.
 Mostly, I want you to know that I am following in your footsteps. I am working hard to become a teacher who touches the lives of her students, just as you did. Thank you for being a role model and thank you for believing in me.
 Love, Megan

After that first mini-lesson in which Megan wrote to her grandfather, each child brainstormed people to whom they could write letters. They each then chose a letter on which to focus for a class publication, a collection of the letters, copied and stapled and placed in the classroom library. Below, I'll share some of the letters children wrote across the years of our inquiry. First, though, let's hone in on Megan's lesson and why we have found this genre to be such a powerful one for inviting children to bring traumatic aspects of life into their school literacies.

In my reading of state and district curricula, I notice that letters aren't included as often in the genres taught in elementary classrooms now as they were in the past (at least in my experience). Letters seem to be folded into other genres, particularly persuasive writing, where writing a letter to argue for something is one form in which argument is taught. I notice they are included in 2nd-grade writing in my state as one of the informational genres children should experience, but at the district level they don't have significant attention in the curricula. Don't get me wrong—in the age of new media and the exciting and ever-expanding forms of communication (from email to texts to social media posts, which are no less valuable than the more formal forms), it can make sense to spend less time on letter-writing per se.

But for our goal to honor children's traumas—their heartbreaks, fears, confusions, longings, and sorting-throughs—my experiences with children's letters suggests it is worth spending even a short time on letter-writing each school year as a context for testimony and witness. And in this genre, I'll be specific about the form your modeled writing can take to open your child witnesses to the possibilities for their own testimonies.

As in Megan's mini-lesson above, it is powerful to write to someone you miss. Further, ensure that it is someone who is physically, materially absent from your life, in whatever form that takes. In other words, write to someone to whom it is impossible (or, at least, complex) to actually send your letter. As with all of our invitations through these pedagogies, children will shape their responses to their own goals. Some will eagerly draft a letter to their best friend sitting across from them at the table in your classroom, or the mom, dad, aunt, or cousin they will see later that day, over the weekend, or at the next family holiday. However, some will bring their own loss to the page. They will burrow into the expressions that writing a letter offers when a teacher's example upends the assumption that it can arrive in the hands of its recipient.

Soon after Megan's modeled letter, Naya wrote this letter draft in her writer's notebook:

Dear Baby Brother,
    I am really sad you died. I wish I can talk to you and I wish you were still alive. It's like you never existed. I want to know if you can

wear mittens. LeShawn, I really miss you. I hope LeShawn, that you really miss me. I want to ask you questions, but you won't reply. I'm feeling happy, but sad because you died. I know you will be in kindergarten. I love you so much. One time I had a dream that you were alive and I was so happy. I really love you.

Naya

I've said it before and I'll say it again, these are words to crawl into, meditate on for a bit, and attempt to absorb for their profundity, their beauty. If you've lost someone dear to you, don't you recognize that tension Naya captures between "it's like you never existed" and that person's ever-presence with you? How her pairing of "I'm feeling happy" and "but sad because you died" captures the sense that happiness is never the absence of sadness, a sensation that is just baked into the everyday of life after such a loss? We can linger on how she weaves wishes like holiday lights throughout her letter. The line "I want to know if you can wear mittens" can be both literal (is baby LeShawn in a tangible place, where mittens can slide onto infant hands?) and metaphorical (the mittens stand for all the mundane moments of life Naya and her baby brother would have shared had he lived). This year, they would have gone to school together, he in kindergarten, she the older sister who could share her wisdom about their school. In her interview about her writing, Naya talked at length about LeShawn, including how she thought of him every time she watched the little kindergartners walking to lunch, to recess, to the library, and wondered what he would have been like.

In that same interview, Naya told me that a "nice teacher" had once told her that her baby brother might not remember her, because "he didn't get to know me before he died." I felt a pang at hearing those words and how they had clearly clung to her. As she revised her letter, though, it became clear that Naya drew on that memory of a former teacher's words to further fuel her writing. In her final letter, she combined elements of her draft letter above with the 10 Things poem from Megan's *Because of Winn-Dixie* poetry mini-lesson. "Here are 10 things about me," she added to her letter to her brother, "My name is Naya, I love you, I am in 2nd grade, I know you want to be here, you are in my head." She repeats several times: "I really miss you." The letter becomes a link between the siblings, the trace of memory, a line of communication in the midst of absence. "If I can talk to you one more time," she writes, "just one more time."

Other children also used their letters to connect amidst their deepest losses. Both Wren and Abran, for instance, wrote to parents who had died.

Dear Dad,
    How are you? I love you. I have been very good. I miss you. I wish I could go up there with you. I really miss you. I can't stop thinking

about you. I am so sad. I wish I could touch you with my finger. I wish you could be down here with me. Mommy misses you too, but I miss you more than anything.
    Love your daughter,
    Wren

When Wren and I talked about her letter to her father, who died when she was a baby, she turned to it, lying between us on the table, and read aloud, "I miss you. I wish I could go up there with you." She paused, "Wait, where is it?" She ran her finger over the words until she found the line she's looking for. "Oh, here it is," and read aloud, "Mommy misses you too but I miss you more than anything." She looked up, "I remember writing in my writing journal 'I don't know you that well, but when I go out there I know I'll know you well.'" She envisioned the reunion she'll someday have, father and daughter recognizing and knowing each other.

That same year, Abran wrote:

Dear Dad,
    I hope I am going to heaven like you did and we could meet roads like me and you were walking by ourselves on a road and you were one block away from me and then I ran up and hugged you.
    Love,
    Abran

Abran's image of two roads converging to bring two people together connects to narratives—both written and filmed—of loss and separation finally resolving as the two figures become discernable to one another in the distance, walking turns to running, and, finally, they are wrapped in joyful embrace. Abran captures that fantasy, longed-for resolution wished by so many who have experienced loss. As in Wren's letter and talk about her father, the image of the longed-for reunion is set in the child's vision of what occurs after death.

I've written about Wren and Abran's letters to their fathers before (Dutro, 2013). There I focused on how, when we engage in conversation with children about a piece of writing they've identified as significant to them, Wren, Abran, and their peers share insights on loss, grief, and memory. Children also describe how they take writing that matters to them from the classroom to other contexts of their lives in ways no teacher could predict or plan for. Both children talked of keeping their letters in their rooms, tangible reminders of their connection to their fathers. As Abran told me, "You know, I can't talk to my dad and so I wrote a letter and I'm, like, seeing if, one day, if I go to heaven, I'll be holding the paper, and I'll be holding the paper, and I'll see him. And I'll be able to say, 'Dad, I wrote this letter to you.' [pause] But, I think he already knows that I wrote to him."

Children's missing of loved ones takes many forms, of course, and several children wrote letters to loved ones they miss who live in other countries, highlighting the ways children carry and nurture transnational connections. Ashika, for instance, often spoke of and wrote about her friends and family in Nepal and wrote to one of those friends in her letter.

> Dear Binsa,
>   I miss you a lot because you have been in Nepal for a long time. Did you know that my mom is having a baby in September? When are you coming anyway? What do you do there anyway?
>   I love you! Love, Ashika

It is far from just geographic distance that suffuses children's writing to the people they love across national borders. Sometimes those communications are inseparable from the personal turmoil imposed by immigration politics and policies. This was true of Clara, whose deep loss and longing is emphasized through her multiple infusions of "I miss you" and "I love you" in her letter to her papa.

> Dear Papa,
>   I wish you and my mom weren't deported because sometimes I miss you when I'm at school. I wish my mom and you can see me because I miss you and I care about you and I can't stop saying I love you because I love you so much.
>   Love, Clara

As with each of the genres I write about in this chapter, I become extra-committed to these practices and pedagogies as I write about them. When we analyzed children's writing in their writer's notebooks, our team found many more letters drafted than had been "required" in this writing unit. With letters, it is simply astounding what children will do when a teacher opens the possibilities of who a letter can be for and how it can travel for its writer.

INFORMATIONAL GENRES

It is interesting to consider how, in elementary literacy curricula, the informational genres are, by definition, new and novel to children (even if they've encountered them since birth). So it is even more striking and (*sigh*) disheartening to consider how many children in the primary grades respond unenthusiastically when I've asked them how they feel about writing in non-narrative genres. How have they had enough time to develop a negative perception of what it means to write in those genres in school? For one clue, I think we can point to how those genres are sometimes approached in writing curricula. For another, we can reflect on our own genre preferences, which may, for some of us, skew toward narrative. When informational writing is framed for us (or by us) as distant from the visceral dimensions of children's lives, it is challenging to consider how to upend those ingrained ideas. But maybe you, like me, have discovered that if you pluck at a thread of those assumptions, they quickly unravel. In my experience the resonance between the stories of our lives and non-narrative genres are often unpredictable, but those connections can be profound.

Cultivating Connection to Informational Topics

When Jade chose "Babies in Their First Year" as her top choice of topic for her 3rd-grade research report, her teacher and I experienced a joint "Of course!" moment. We knew that Jade's adored big sister, 12 years old, was 4 months pregnant. Jade was keeping me closely posted about the fetus's development, and just that week of topic choosing, her sister had felt the first tiny-wing flutter of those fast-forming limbs. Jade was taking her role as future auntie very seriously. She wanted to know how this little one was going to grow and change—and what she could do to help this baby along its way. After all, her sister was a primary caretaker in her life, as her mother worked night shifts to keep them in their apartment. For the month of that writing unit, every book she plucked from the library shelf, every login at the computer lab, was a quest of anticipation, of joy, of commitment. They could do this, keep this baby safe and strong—two little girls and their mother, who, in her own words, was "overwhelmed."

In Jade's case, the importance of her topic in her current life was clear. And we can see how the term trauma may apply in Jade's sister's situation. If the baby's father is an adult, it is abuse or assault that led to her pregnancy. If it is another child, we might imagine he is caught up in something huger than he likely imagined would occur in his preteen or adolescent life. As much love and adoration as this baby was sure to receive, we may imagine it will be difficult for this family, already struggling just to keep the utilities running, to support another person. But her experience also reveals that crucial idea from Chapter 3 (and that we know in our bones from our own experiences): The hard stuff cannot be extracted, sometimes, from the comfort and the joy.

I was in Jade's classroom a few days a week for the full school year and remember the research report unit well. I was attuned to her and her classmates' choices of topics for their research reports: German Shepherds, Mexican holidays, Louisiana, trains, a local body of water, tornadoes, to name just a few. Each chosen topic had a reason that mattered, in various ways, to the writer who chose it. Each topic had a story about *why* it was chosen. What was I *not* as attuned to at the time? Although I was heeding the writers' topics and their reasons for choosing them, I wasn't attending closely to what was allowing those "why stories" to exist. The answer is both simple and sublime. And I'm sure you already know what I'm about to say. Personal topic choice! Being able to choose their own topics to dig into meant that the room was full of children's stories of the reasons for their choices.

You've no doubt seen or experienced a writing curriculum that included common topics for informational genres. And you can sense the conversations of the well-meaning and highly informed adults who designed it. I imagine someone pointing to how it will ease the burden on the teacher. I imagine another person emphasizing how a common topic allows teachers to more easily compare children to one another. It allows for joint inquiry, which can certainly be productive. There might be a bit of push-back at the table: If we don't allow for topic choice, we need to ensure that it is a topic all children will be interested in. Vehicles! Extreme weather! Animals of all kinds!

And realistically, offering students their choice of topics will be impossible in some curricular contexts. In that case, it is important to find any wiggle room we can for children to feel investment in their research topics. The topics I just listed could allow for choice within those categories ("animals" is huge and there will be lions, tigers, and bears, oh my!). But what there won't be, in any of those examples, is Jade's opportunity to investigate "Babies in Their First Year."

When I think of my own experiences as a student, hands-down my favorite university courses were those where we were given the leeway to bring our own topics and intellectual passions to our final papers. I tolerated those that were more directive, but I just couldn't relish my learning in the same way. This reminds me of an idea that is so common it is difficult to know exactly who to credit with the words that often capture it: Research is often deeply connected to autobiography. In some way or another, the topics to which people devote their life's work connect to circumstances of their lives. Just like the children in Marie's classroom and yours, those rationales will vary widely—a fascination with bugs for as long as she can remember, parents who risked everything to cross the U.S. southern border, a childhood illness that meant months spent in the hospital. But, bottom line: Ask writers and researchers about their "why story" and you're likely in for a lengthy conversation.

Although I am arguing for the importance of topic choice as a means to support students who are bringing difficult experiences into the classroom, research has long provided many reasons for why meaningful and personal topic choice is important in writing. For our purposes here, we will gather up those crucial reasons and infuse attention to trauma. For decades studies have shown that choosing topics that matter to individual students fuels motivation, engagement, and investment (e.g., Graves, 1983; Haddix, 2009; Murray, 1991). If students are invested in what they are doing, they are more likely to see school as a place and a process worth investing in, as well as to have more sustained practice with school writing across genres (e.g., Dyson, 2003; Paris & Alim, 2017). In short, research suggests choice, agency, and connection in school literacies as an important aspect of teaching in inclusive, relevant, and sustaining ways that honor racial, cultural, class, and gender histories and identities of children (e.g., Genishi & Dyson, 2015; Ghiso, 2016; Ryan & Hermann-Wilmarth, 2018).

In addition to those crucial reasons, topic choice opens an invitation to make a research report matter to a complex aspect of life that exists on some spectrum of what may be deemed trauma. Allowing Jade and her classmates to choose what to investigate and write about propelled her and some of her classmates to focus on topics related to what I knew to be a range of complexities and challenges in their lives. Others enjoyed choosing topics that mattered to them, but didn't connect to difficult experiences, whether or not they were in the midst of something hard.

Topic choice is just one part, if an important one, of opening space for difficult experiences to be included and honored as fertile ground for informational writing. In this genre, too, a teacher's testimony and intentional modeling open an invitation for children to bring a full range of connections—memory, loss, relationships, struggle—to their writing. No matter the topic, no matter the constrictions teachers may need to navigate in a given curriculum, our own stories and the ways we share them in literacy instruction are always there as a crucial resource. As illustrated in the examples below, bringing testimony to informational genres opens possibilities for writers to craft a "why story" that provides one more way for school literacies to matter to a writer's life. Below I share examples of testimony and critical witness pedagogies in the context of research reports and persuasive writing, two of the informational genres we regularly teach in elementary literacy.

Opening Space for Life Connections

In Marie's classroom, the research report project launched with a lesson in which Marie shared her own contemplations of topics she might choose to research and why she was drawn to them. In other words, it was a lesson on topic choice, which is often included near the start of genre units. I describe that lesson below, drawing on the detailed notes that I took while it was happening.

In Marie's large city school district at the time, most writing instruction was integrated into the district's adopted literacy curriculum, which, although it included some attention to listening, speaking, and writing, was heavily weighted toward reading. Marie was a White woman in her 50s who had entered teaching as a second phase of her professional life and had been teaching for about 10 years. As she described, since she started teaching the literacy program adoption was by far the most mandated and monitored curricular experience she'd encountered. District instructional leaders visited classrooms at Marie's school about once a month and they expected to see all teachers at the pre-designated place in the curriculum. It was a high-stress situation for Marie and other teachers, and she didn't feel the space or permission to do much innovating or improvising within the literacy curriculum.

Although some writing accompanied each unit, it didn't allow for a full writer's workshop model. For the unit focused on reading and writing for research, though, quite a bit of time was allotted for children to investigate and write their own research reports. Since the topic wasn't specified, Marie took advantage of the flexibility and supported children to choose their own topics.

The day she launched the research unit, Marie stood in front of the room with a chart paper easel on her right. She launched her lesson with a big smile and, in an enthusiastic voice, told the children they were all going to get to research a topic of interest and write about it. "Just imagine," she said, "you can choose something that matters to *you*. There are so many things you might choose!" She explained that they would get to start thinking about their topics today, but first she wanted to share with them what she thought about when she was considering topics that she might want to research. "I ask myself, 'What is something that is really important to me?' 'What is something I can imagine reading and writing about for the next 2 weeks and not get tired of it at all?'" On the chart paper, she wrote, "Things to think about when I choose a research topic" and wrote her two considerations as bullets beneath the heading.

She shared that she'd immediately thought of some of her favorite activities and hobbies. She wrote "My Topics" on the chart paper too, ready for her list of possibilities. "I thought about baking. There are some interesting things to find out about the history of certain kinds of bread or the kinds of ovens people used way before humans had electricity." She explained that she had memories of baking with her mother on holidays and that she used those recipes with her own daughter. She went on, "I also thought about cats. You know I love my two cats and it would be interesting to know more about how humans came to have cats as pets or just to understand all the different kinds of cats and their characteristics." She mentioned the painter Monet, as he was her favorite artist, and she added his name to her list of possible topics. Finally, she wrote "trains" on her list. She paused, and when she spoke her voice was wistful. It's strange, she told the children, that even writing the word "train" brings so many memories. "When I was a kid," she said, "we lived near train tracks and every night, right around my bedtime, I'd hear the train rattling down the tracks. But most important to me are my memories of my grandpa, who knew a lot about trains. Every time he came to visit, he and I would walk down to the train tracks and he would tell me facts and stories about trains. Sometimes, on the luckiest days, we'd get to be there when a train went by. It's like I can still feel that rush of air that would hit my face because the train was going by fast. Usually they were coal trains, but sometimes they were carrying animals, mostly cows, and I would try to glimpse their cow faces through the little slits in the cattle cars as they sped by." She drew a circle around "trains" with her purple marker. She looked at the children with a small, melancholy smile. "I am choosing trains. My grandpa died when I was 12 and even just thinking about trains makes me think of him and how special he was to me. I definitely want to research something about trains. I will need to think about what to focus on about that topic, but at least I know my topic." She then turned to the transition from lesson to independent writing. "Now, you will all make a list of *your* possible topics, think about why you might want to focus on those things, and choose the one that you feel most excited to think about and learn more about."

As you might imagine, the range of individual topics that the children chose fell into some larger categories, including animals and insects, states or countries, geographical features, human biology and physiology, cultural practices, and transportation. When I think about children's topics through the lens of deep connections to children's lives, I see even more clearly now how Marie's initial lesson mattered to what children explored in their reports. A child investigated how smoking effects the heart because his grandpa was recovering from a heart attack. A child chose German Shepherds because her great-uncle had one that she loved when she was "a little kid" and the dog had died the year before. Looking back, I also think about Julian's topic, which was related to the history of a local park. Julian is the child who appears in the first pages of this book, who had lost his baby brother. Julian's story of why he chose his topic focused on his family's time at the park—for picnics and birthday parties—and I can imagine now how happy times as a family connect to the immense loss he lives with and the positive memories the family continues to build together.

Persuasive and opinion writing also opens up opportunities for children to connect to significant life experiences, including trauma. Ellie Haberl (2019) has done powerful work on the connections young writers can make between deeply meaningful, often challenging, life experiences and persuasive writing. In her study, she and Michael, a 7th-grade classroom teacher, planned a persuasive writing unit that sought to muddy the boundaries between personal narrative and persuasive writing genres. She describes how she felt the pull of her own experience in the issues and ideas about which she would wish to form arguments. She wondered how middle school students would respond to opportunities to make those connections.

Ellie and Michael launched the persuasive writing unit with personal narratives focused on small moments (Calkins & Oxenhorn, 2003). The students then drew from their small moments to choose topics for their persuasive essays. Crucially, and in the spirit of the pedagogies I am championing in this book, Ellie and Michael each modeled their personal narrative small moments before the students wrote their own. Each teacher deliberately chose to focus on a challenging aspect of life, a story that felt vulnerable to share. Ellie wrote of family members' struggles with addiction. Michael shared about the death of his father.

Curricula may suggest that genres exist in columns. Instead, we can think of them existing in a web. Lorenzo's published poem in 2nd grade is titled "Bats" and is full of facts about bats he learned from the informational text he features as the repeated refrain of his poem ("I learned that from a bat book called *Flying Bats*"). Wren, who I introduced earlier through her letter to her father who had died when she was an infant, wrote this entry in her writer's notebook called "Non Fiction Angel" during the time the class was writing informational texts:

I saw an angel in the sky. It would show its face when I looked at it and when I would try to talk to it, it would talk in a suspicious voice. His voice sounded like dad and his face looked like my dad. And I was wondering if he was my dad. My mom would say you would get to see him one day and I could always hear him call my name. The End.

She uses her understanding of the genre to assert the fact of her father's presence in angelic form. This angel, she asserts in her title, is not fiction, not imaginary. This was a belief she consistently (and poetically) expressed in her writing and in conversations about her writing across genres and contexts.

The parameters of standards and assessments very often require that informational writing stick to strict conventions of genre. We can embrace that children are well-served by learning genre conventions. However, we can also challenge the notion that informational genres are not and cannot be deeply connected with, and influenced by, the most important stories of our lives, including the hardest ones. The bottom line is that our pedagogy and the connections that *teachers* share in instruction about why informational text matters to *you* shake up falsely rigid boundaries between genres. It is creative and vibrant work to delve deep into your own stories and find those meaningful connections to any given topic a curriculum can toss at you. Children will respond.

NARRATIVE GENRES

For while the tale of how we suffer, and how we are delighted, and how we may triumph is never new, it always must be heard. There isn't any other tale to tell, it's the only light we've got in all this darkness.

—James Baldwin ("Sonny's Blues")

Baldwin's words can fuel our commitments to craft our literacy classrooms in ways that provide opportunity for children to tell their stories—and have them heard. Research across disciplines reminds us that humans are narratively driven beings (e.g., Bruner, 1991; Moraga & Anzaldúa, 1981; Ochs & Capps, 2001). We live, tell, seek, and encounter stories everywhere, all the time. Narrative gives shape and meaning to the worlds we inhabit.

So it is well worth spending additional time with narrative as a central context for honoring the knowledge, and the pain, wrought of difficult experiences in children's lives. I first discuss children's fiction writing as a context for teachers to glean insights into the inventive, subtle ways children weave their most impactful experiences into their imaginary tales. I then turn to two additional illustrations of enacting testimony and witness in personal narrative writing instruction. In the first example, the focus of the lesson is published literature as a mentor text. In the second, Megan's modeled personal narrative serves as the mentor text. We'll also see how Megan embedded invitations for children to write about difficult experiences with attention to the district curriculum and the accompanying rubric for the unit.

Fiction

One afternoon I was sitting with Leo talking with him about his writing. Although his 3rd-grade class was working on personal narratives, he explained that he wasn't writing a personal narrative. He wanted to write a different kind of story. He said he knew the personal narrative he would write, but he didn't want to tell his story that way. The story he *was* writing was about a baby with magic powers who was taken away by an evil ghost. "Actually," he told me, "it's like my own story because *I* was taken away from my mom for a while when I was a baby. But it's about this magical baby and instead of the woman who took me away, it's about an evil ghost." "Wow," I said, "so you are doing what some of the best fiction writers do. You're drawing on your own experience to write a fictional story." "Yeah," he said. "It's kind of based on me, but it's not me."

When Leo wrote his fictional story, the connections to this pillar experience of his separation from his mother would be far from obvious to most of his readers. Those links, though, were the genesis and foundation of his fictional story. For Leo, the borders between stories drawn from life and narrative fiction genres were explicitly blurred in how he was opting to participate in his writing curriculum's focus on narrative that day. As he read his tale to me, everything in his body language spoke to his pride in what he'd accomplished.

Were you Leo's teacher, you could potentially access the connections between his creative writing and the life experiences he was pulling into his fiction. However, it's not a given that we see and trace those threads, even if most of us would wish to. We can imagine a response that frames him as writing in the wrong genre, refusing to engage with our instructional goals, and ignoring our instructions. But right there below the surface of what might seem obvious and simple to identify is a rich complexity of how Leo is thinking about genres and their relationship to what is "true."

Insights into how children will often draw from threads of life in their fictional texts require our intentional reflection and analysis. The seams between trauma and fairy tales, folktales, and realistic fiction stories can so often remain invisible. But when we hone our curiosities, bring our questions, listen deeply, and pull out our magnifying glass and linger over children's writing across genres—there they are.

Personal Narrative

Published Author as Mentor Text. As the children gathered on the rug at the front of the room and turned their eyes to Megan, she settled into her low purple chair and reached for the mentor text she had chosen for this personal narrative mini-lesson: *Visiting Day* by Jacqueline Woodson. Woodson's picture book recounts the experience of a girl who visits her father in prison. Megan read the book with her usual vibrant, expressive voice and paused several times to discuss ideas, vocabulary, author's craft, and to acknowledge and listen to children who chimed in or raised a hand to share a connection to the story. That day, three children shared that they too had a family member in prison. After the reading and discussion, Megan explained to the children:

Megan: "Here's what we're going to do today. I don't know exactly what it's like. I have never known anyone to go to jail, but I have felt really sad before. And I have missed people a lot. I'm going to give you an invitation to write. If this book helped you remember something that happened in your own life, I'm inviting you, today, to write about that."

Jessica: "You mean kind of like a heart poem except it's a personal narrative?"

Megan (nodding at Jessica): "Maybe you want to write about somebody who didn't go to jail, but maybe they left for a long time. And if this story didn't make you think about anything in your life, I'm inviting you to write about something else that has happened to you.

"Then we'll spend some time at the end of writer's workshop seeing, does our story match what it says it's about? Do we use conventions?" (She gestures to the poster-size rubric beside her.)

Megan: "Share with your elbow buddy what you can write about today." (The children turn to their neighbors and share their ideas.)

Megan (after counting down from five to signal children to finish their partner sharing): "How many of you think this story helped you remember a pretty important story? [Many hands go up.] How many of you think you want to write about something different? [Several hands go up.] So, we have some kids who will write about something connected to *Visiting Day* and some kids who will write about something different."

Notice how Megan explicitly positions herself in relation to the story. She is very clear that she doesn't share this experience. She then zooms out to connect to the larger themes and feelings conveyed in the book with which she does connect. Throughout this book, I've emphasized the idea of *invitation,* never requirement, for children to bring their difficult experiences to their classroom literacies. This excerpt from Megan's lesson shows how to make that distinction explicit and clear to children. The options to pursue writing connected in some way to resonance with the book or to write about something not at all related are validated before children leave the rug to write their narratives. Megan underscored children's choice and agency within her invitation each time she engaged testimony and witness in her instruction.

Also, we see how Megan folded attention to conventions and other aspects of the writing rubric from the district curriculum into her transition from mini-lesson to independent writing. In this and the example below, we can see how to attend to a caution that I raised in Chapter 2: If we reify challenging life experiences as outside the realm of academic work in literacy classrooms, those experiences will be marginalized as resources for children. Trauma can be deeply honored and met with love, empathy, and support *and* be the context for children to pursue learning goals.

When the children moved to their desks to write, the three children who shared their connection with Woodson's book in the mini-lesson wrote about their family members in prison. Others wrote about family members that they missed, including loved ones who had died, a parent and an uncle who they rarely got to see, friends and family who have moved away, and a separation forced by deportation. Still others readily took up the invitation to focus on something less explicitly connected to *Visiting Day*, writing about a fun weekend outing or playing a game with their cousins.

Teacher-Modeled Writing as Mentor Text. A few days after their experience with *Visiting Day*, the children gathered as usual on the rug for the start of writer's workshop. Megan's mini-lesson focused on a modeled narrative about the day she found out that her grandfather passed away. As the lesson launched, Megan told the children that the story she was going to write that day was inspired by the stories three children wrote after the class read *Visiting Day*.

Megan: "Today, I'm going to write about the time my grandfather passed away. He was very close to me, very special. This was my Dad's dad. I called him Papa. (She turned to the chart paper and held her pen poised at the top of the page.) So, let's say, I'm gonna name it . . . (She paused and looked from the page to the children.) Gosh, I don't know. . . It happened in August."

Some of the children voiced ideas for possible titles and Megan nodded thoughtfully at each idea.

Juan: "My Saddest Time of All"

Emma: "Shocking News"

Megan: "Hmmm. I think just 'The Sad Day.' I might go back and change it because sad is kind of a boring word.

Jessica: "What about 'The Tragic Day?'

Megan: "Hmmm. Tragic. I'm not sure it was tragic. Maybe it was. Tragic is a great adjective. But I'm going to think about it, if that's okay."

Megan then began to write her opening to the narrative: It was a sunny, warm August afternoon. My sister . . .

Jossalyn (interjects): "Katherine"

Megan: "You know what, that's probably better than saying 'my sister' since you know her name." (She crossed out "my sister," wrote "Katherine," and continued writing.) *"Katherine and I were inside trying to stay cool."*

Megan paused to read aloud what she had written so far.

Megan: "When I write about something like this, when I'm remembering what happened, I feel kind of sad. Does that ever happen to you? When I got this news, I got this really sick feeling in my stomach."

Emma: "Did you cry?"

Megan: "I did cry. I get the sick feeling, again. Did you ever get that feeling?"

As she drafted her narrative, she continued to talk aloud about the decisions she was making as a writer, periodically pausing to seek and respond to children's ideas—about word choice, punctuation, and what she might want to change when she revised. When she had filled two pages of the chart paper, she stopped.

Megan: "So, I'm going to stop there for today, but let's go to my rubric. Where was I for my content?"

Several children: "4!"

Megan: "4's are kind of reserved for published books. So, I would say it's a 3. My title said, 'The Sad Day.' Did I write about the sad day? What about my conventions?"

Again, pointing to the rubric, Megan talked about her conventions, pointing to specific examples of spelling, punctuation, and indented paragraphs. She then transitioned the children to independent writing.

Megan: "We have lots of time today to write. Thank you very much for being respectful while I shared that hard story with you. Today I'm going to invite you, again. If there's something you want to write about that was sad in your life, kind of like I wrote about with my papa, you can write about that. It doesn't have to be about someone dying—maybe your pet got lost and ran away. But maybe there was a time you had that feeling in your stomach, too. But you don't have to. You can write about something from the weekend, something silly that happened, etc."

In this example, we see many of the same moves as in the previous lesson—explicit emphasis on invitation and clearly conveyed options of what a writer may choose to pursue. Here Megan shared her own experience in ways that positioned children as witnesses, invited them into her writing process, and described the way her body feels as she writes about a hard memory of loss. She also modeled how a story that deeply matters to the writer can be a context for revising, editing, and making writing stronger.

Analyzing the writing that the children took up after Megan's modeled personal narrative showed the multiple ways that Megan's narrative served as a mentor text for children. Many children wrote about loss, feelings of sorrow, or the moment of hearing hard news, connecting to the content and themes of her narrative. In addition, many children wove craft elements from Megan's story into their own. In the examples I share below, each child's narrative connected in novel and personalized ways to Megan's narrative about her grandfather's death and/or Woodson's *Visiting Day* in both theme and form.

Following Megan's modeled narrative, Haley also wrote a narrative about learning of her grandfather's death, and her title, "The Saddest Day," echoes Megan's. She wrote: "It was a cold day and I was sad. I knew a part of me was missing. My aunt called." In her narrative that day, Lizzie wrote: "I was at home watching a movie and my mom said she was going to my aunt's house. She came back and started crying because my aunt passed away. I started crying too because she used to give me everything I wanted and she was my favorite of all my aunts." Julianna's narrative, "My Grandpa Died," doesn't linger on how she learns of her grandpa's death, but instead captures the stretching of time in some experiences of loss. She wrote, "I went with my dad to the hospital! I wasn't allowed to see him for a long time. He died. We went to the funeral for a lot of days. We dug him in the dirt. I felt sad for a long time."

Other children's narratives took up themes of loss and separation that connected to themes in both Megan's modeled narrative and Woodson's *Visiting Day*. Ariella, for instance, wrote about the last time she saw her father before he left the family. "5 years ago was probably the last time I got to see my dad. I was 3. I thought I'd see him for longer than 1 week. When we got home, my mom told me he took everything she didn't care about. He had left me behind! My mom said we never *needed* him. But I loved him and realized we didn't. And those are some memories of my Dad." Given that she was 3 when her father left, her memories may or may not be very clear, but she carries them and the stories she's been told about him and his presence in her life. Her line "He had left me behind!" holds poignant double meanings in this writer's story—both a cry of pain of being left and affirmation of her mother's care for her (he took only the things her mother didn't care about).

Over the 3 years of our inquiry, Woodson's *Visiting Day*, coupled with Megan's explicit invitations to bring the full range of life experiences to school literacies, consistently resulted in some children's writing about family members' incarceration. After the mini-lesson with *Visiting Day*, Tonya wrote a personal narrative titled "My Uncle was in Jail": "When I was 5 years old, my uncle was in jail. I only got to see him 2 times a month. So, I was really sad because that was a little bit. When we went again, we played some games because my mom was talking to my uncle. He was playing with us too." She writes in the past tense about her experience of her uncle's time in prison, a time she implicitly contrasts to his frequent presence in her life before and since that time.

It's also important to know the other variations in how children responded to Megan's testimony in her narrative. Amelia, for instance, drew on Megan's title, but shifted a key word. Her story, "The Happy Day," recounts the day her sister came home for a visit. "It was such a happy day!" And in the persistent theme of pets in children's lives, Mateo wrote the story, "The Saddest Sad Sad Day." Like many of his classmates', his title is a version of Megan's. "One sunny day," his story starts, also an echo of his teacher's first line, "I went to go feed my turtle Joey. Then we saw her eat. I went to go eat something and I went back. My turtle was not moving. I fed her food. She did not eat it. I felt her throat. She wasn't breathing. So my dad went to throw her in the trash can. I was so so so sad. My stomach was aching." Mateo's story reverberates from Megan's—his title, the lightness of the sun contrasting with the weight of shocking sadness, the ache in the body. He takes up the invitation by writing about his turtle in a way that reveals how easy it is for adults to underestimate the weight of pet loss. That turtle, Joey, appears over and over in Mateo's writing, and I'll return to Mateo in the next chapter.

I share these examples of children's writing that followed Megan's infusion of testimony—her own writing and Woodson's—to demonstrate the various ways children responded to these explicit invitations to bring loss and other forms of trauma into their school literacies. Although, as we've seen, all genres offer important opportunities for those invitations, personal narrative offers particularly powerful contexts for engaging in reciprocal witnessing with children.

REFLECTIONS ON GENRE AND CHILDREN'S TRAUMAS

I entered my inquiries into the swirl of trauma, literacies, testimony, vulnerability, reciprocity, and critical witness with a crystal-clear assumption about the importance of personal narrative and poetry in opportunities to make the hard parts of life matter in literacy classrooms. I'd seen it and written about it before. However, prior to these inquiries with children and their committed, skillful teachers, I didn't fully understand how invitations to weave life and literacies can and must be infused across genres in literacy classrooms.

In the next chapter, we'll see how children weave their lives—including the knowledge and perspectives they've gleaned from experiences of trauma—into their literacies across their school year. We'll notice how children's responses to invitations to bring trauma to their literacies come in shimmers, rather than spotlights, embers floating away from the flame, rather than the bonfire. We can pursue those sparks, keep them in sight, like trailing a firefly through a July-warm evening,

FOR REFLECTION, DISCUSSION, AND PRACTICE

- Approach children's writing across genres as you would poetry.
  - » Read for metaphor, imagery, striking turns of phrase.
  - » If you find yourself struggling to see beyond conventions, transcribe the child's writing with conventional grammar and spelling so you can focus on the meaning and use of literary devices and the flow and structure of the language.
- Write a letter to someone you miss, in whatever way you miss them. It can and should be a letter you can't or won't ever be able to send.
  - » What does it hold that you might be able to share with your students?
- Consider your own connections to informational genres.
  - » Take any given informational genre and topic that might appear in literacy curricula and consider how you could connect to it, launch it through your own testimony, and present your own story of why that topic is important to you.
  - » Then imagine topics that you would most want to investigate, read about, and write about. Here, too, consider how you can turn your connection to topics into a story to share with children. This process can help us see the ways both prescribed topics and choice are opportunities for investment and deep personal connection.

CHAPTER 5

Tracing Children's Testimonies to Trauma Across the School Year

I wonder how long it was before we went back to Taco Tia, our all-time favorite burrito joint, the Wednesday family tradition. My family moved to Redlands, California, in the very late 1970s when Taco Tia was still a small stand, just off of a main thoroughfare. You walked up to a counter, placed your order—3 green burritos, 1 red, 4 tostadas—and waited on the sidewalk until it was handed to you through the window. We were familiar with the two women who were always at the counter (who I remember as middle-aged, but who knows, they may have been all of 30), familiar because we came so often, like clockwork, and because my mother connects with people once she's been back anywhere more than a few times. Each week, some smiles and chitchat, confirming "the usual."

In May 1983, when it's weeks before we're back, do they wonder about us? When we do return, they do seem to have wondered, looking at my mother with concern, but no prying questions. She needs to tell them, wants to tell them, so her eyes fill and overflow, and I'm struck, standing on the edge of it all, that their eyes fill too. One woman says something about the beautiful boy as she hands us our lighter, still-warm bag.

And we resume. We're there again, each and every week, and it continues through the end of high school, each weekend of college, folding in the two new little siblings, the ones Kenny never got to know; and, with my future husband now part of the pattern, I was still there, every week, during my first 2 years of teaching in the city nearby. Now, although my family and I have long since moved away, I still go to Taco Tia once or twice a year with my own children when we return to that town to visit my mother-in-law. We unpack the fat, warm, heavy burritos onto her plastic table-clothed kitchen table, passing around the drinks, laughing, chatting, relishing the time-traveling flavor. And, always or almost always, on one day of the visit, I sneak away, drive alone to the now shabby, larger, eat-in building Taco Tia expanded into while my brother was not there to see its transformation. I order my burrito and drive to the cemetery, up the so-familiar winding road at the top of that town. I sit under the tree, grown so impossibly stately from that gangly adolescence of our first introduction, peeling back the white paper wrapper, sinking my teeth into that particular softness. This is the taste of memory. This is the tribute to the small and significant everyday details of a shared life. That's all. Eating memories is one of those common tropes beautifully captured again and again in poems, novels, films, memoirs—because it is what it is. The taste of what is missed.

* * *

What is missed. In her poem, "Aunt Died," Martina includes the refrain "I am missing her," following lines about what is missing. "Letters, written to my mom and dad telling us she is missing us. . . . Stories, telling me about my mom when she was a little girl." The day Megan shared her personal narrative about her grandfather's death, Martina recounted the moment she found out her aunt had died. She takes her readers into the launch of a day in which she woke up happy, took a shower, watched TV, heard her mother cooking in the kitchen—and then "the phone rang, 'ring ring.'" At a later point in her notebook, Martina wrote another narrative that subtly reverberates from the death of her aunt, describing a day when "it looked like our mom was sad, but I cheered her up." Examined as separate, the way Martina's mother's sadness radiates from the story of her sister's recent death could easily be lost. But, read carefully across a year's worth of Martina's writing, her notebook paints a vivid portrait of an aunt's love and a child's grief.

Certain difficult, life-altering experiences are pillar events at various times in our lives. It is true for adults and certainly true for children. In this chapter we'll see how children weave significant life events, including trauma, into their literacies across the school year. Delving deep into individual children's writing and talk across time illuminates the nuanced and often subtle ways children respond to invitations to bring the challenging experiences of their lives to their literacies. In other words, the impact of invitations to make trauma matter to literacy learning are not always immediately obvious and require us to take a long view.

Tracing how children bring trauma to their literacies over time also provides a crucial context to attend to the critical in critical witnessing. We can notice how inequitable systems and policies impact children who are targeted because of race, class, gender, language, and when and how they or their families arrived in the United States. My hope is that we can take this chapter as another opportunity to hone heart-centered, justice-vigilant analysis to uncover the vast knowledge, some borne of trauma, that children bring to their literacies.

CHILDREN WEAVING TESTIMONY INTO LITERACIES OVER TIME

I turn now to how several children over the years of our inquiry wove particular pillar experiences into the literacy curriculum across their school year in Megan's classroom.

Enrique

When I first met Enrique, he whispered his question, "Which one are we doing now?," so softly that I crouched lower by his desk and leaned in close to be sure I heard it right. As soon as I said the class was starting their drawings of a silly experience on the personal narrative topics sheet, he nodded and bent over his paper. Enrique was a calm, often quiet presence in the classroom. On the rug, his eyes were most often riveted to whatever Megan was doing in her mini-lessons. He volunteered his ideas verbally sometimes, if not often, and seemed comfortable when Megan asked if he would share his ideas. He was socially well-connected in his classroom and with other 2nd-grade peers, always interacting with friends on the playground and in the lunchroom.

In the early days of winter, Enrique drafted and published this poem.

"My Cousin Miguel Died"
My cousin Miguel died.
He was my bestest cousin
Of all my other cousins.
I don't know why he died
But I will keep him in one place
My heart.
I'll always keep him there.
I'll never take him out.

—Enrique

He wrote his poem after Megan's mini-lesson that used *Because of Winn-Dixie* as a poetry mentor text. This was the lesson, shared in detail in Chapter 4, when she shared her experience of missing Jonah, the dog she had not seen since the end of a relationship the year before. This was the first time Enrique had written about his cousin's death. However, it was not the first time his cousin had appeared in Enrique's writing. Miguel was a central presence, as was loss. However, the fullness of Enrique's response to invitations to bring his grief to his school literacies is only apparent through looking at the arc of Enrique's writing throughout the fall, to the moment of the winter poem, and into the spring.

Early in the fall, Enrique's cousin appears first on his "seed list" of topics he might write about for a personal narrative, the first writing unit of the year:

My Cousin Miguel died
I broke my arm
Uncle, grandmother died
I tripped and hit the side of my chin
Baby chickens died

Enrique was in Megan's class during the fall in which she taught the lemons and lemonade personal narrative unit that I shared in Chapter 3. In addition to *The Lemonade Club* as an anchor mentor text, Megan had shared narratives about her parents' separation when she was a child and her grandfather's death. From his list of possible topics, Enrique includes difficult experiences, including death and loss, as well as injury. The narrative he chose to write about as his "lemon," though, was the last idea on his list: the deaths of baby chickens:

One time my family baby chickens died. Some were lonely, that's how some died. And some got attacked and some didn't make it out of their shell. Then I dried them. Take very good care of them, I heard my mom praying to god. I quickly ran to see why she was praying. Then I saw her praying to the chicken that was dying.

His narrative conveys multiple dimensions of death and loss. He evokes the finality of death, the multiple risks baby chicks faced that led to their deaths, and the care and prayers that couldn't save them. Is it reading too much into his focus on loneliness as a matter of life and death to connect that to his missing of Miguel? That's for each reader to decide. For me, he captures something resonant with my own sense of the dire loneliness of loss.

In another entry from that fall, right around Halloween, Enrique conveys a memory from the year before.

One night I went to a high school or a middle school and I dressed up as a ninja. It had a dragon on my costume and my cousin dressed up as a ninja too and his costume had a dragon on his costume too except his was black. Mine was red and black. Mine and my cousin's costume were almost the same and people at the high school or middle school said that my costume was cool and they said that my cousin's costume was cool too. It was the best night of my life.

This memory of that last Halloween with Miguel is connected to grief in ways that cannot be accessed without encountering the poem written months later and reading them in conjunction with one another.

Connections to Miguel run through other pages of his notebook, extending into spring. When Enrique makes a list of possible letter recipients or focus for fiction later in the year, cousins and Miguel and a grandmother who has died are the first three on this list. He then lists several family members' names, as well as "break dancing," "dancing," and "first communion." The length of Enrique's writer's notebook also matters, as he is one of the children who fills relatively few pages across the school year. Thus, the ratio of drafts and entries that connect in important ways to loss and, specifically, the loss of his cousin, is high.

Next to his draft of the story of the baby chickens dying, Enrique has an arrow pointing to a space across the page, where he writes, "this is a lemon for me because I never had an animal or pet die in my family." His recent experience of having a beloved family member die is a shadow story to the one about the baby chicks, his Halloween memory, and other writings completed before and after the poem that explicitly delves into Miguel's death. The significance of this explanation for why this is a lemon story, and the exploration of loss that runs through that story, requires a school-year-long perspective to fully absorb.

Mateo

Some children responded to pedagogies of testimony and critical witness across their school year by tracing difficult experiences that were clearly salient in their lives, even if the experience might not meet common assumptions of what counts as trauma. In Chapter 4 I included Mateo's story, "The Saddest Sad Sad Day," about discovering his pet turtle, Joey, had died—a narrative he modeled after Megan's personal narrative, "The Sad Day," about the day she learned her grandfather had died. Later in the personal narrative unit, Mateo wrote another personal narrative, "The New Pet," which starts with the same opening phrase, "One sunny day," as his first narrative, both echoing Megan's first line. He wrote,

> One sunny day me and my whole family, we had 250 dollars so we thought it will be nice to buy a puppy. We went to a person's house. They ask if you wanted a puppy. We all said yes. Then we went back to the car. We were all thinking of a name for it. We all named it Chiqui. We went to buy a bowl then we all bought a bed.

The narrative Mateo wrote next also focused on a pet, this time his pet turtle again. In "The Number One Pet" he writes, "One sunny day I went home when school was over. I went to my room. I saw something green and swimming. I looked at it. It was a turtle. My mom told me we bought a pet. I was happy." Earlier in the year Mateo had written a poem that included stanzas on both pets. This was the poem he selected to publish for the class book.

Chiqui
Sitting on a brown couch staring at me
Moving her little tongue with her mouth
She is kind of good at tricks
But the only things she likes to do is bite my brother's pants
She is nice to me
She likes to see people
Sometimes she is crazy
I think she likes walks, and sometimes she tried to run
Sometimes we have to carry her when she is tired
She likes to eat toilet paper and have fun.
Joey
I'm sad because you are not alive anymore
I can see you in my dreams
And I can see you in my window in my imagination
I will never forget you, not even once
I will never forget you.

As a collection of writing, the joy of the new puppy is inseparable from the loss of Joey the turtle. His three narratives convey the complexity of loss for Mateo: his sadness at Joey's death, excitement about the puppy, and then a kind of re-emphasis on Joey's significance as "the number one pet." His poem then brings the two together on the page. Mateo's writing serves as another illustration of how children took up invitations to testify to meaningful events in their lives, and defined for themselves what counted as the experiences that they would bring to the page.

Carlton and Sonia

We first met Carlton in Chapter 3. Second grade launched with his converging experiences of being removed from his biological family and a recent lymphoma diagnosis. His experience was a catalyst for Megan's commitment to diving deeply into pedagogies of testimony and witness to trauma in her 2nd year of teaching. Here I return to Carlton to show how the complex cluster of traumas in his life travel through literacies across time, not just in his own year in Megan's classroom, but also 2 years later when his little sister entered Megan's class. I focus on the siblings' writer's notebooks, but want to remind us of the ways Carlton shared about his illness in other contexts as well, including the morning meetings that served as spaces for community-building in Megan's classroom.

Reading through Carlton's writer's notebook, his illness and separation from his biological family are explicit or implicit presences in many of his entries. He started his notebook with two pages devoted to his belief in God. He wrote, "I love God. He is a hero" on the first page and "I love God because he is making me feel better" on the second. As a witness to Carlton's school year and reader of his writing, I can almost hear all of the pleas to God, his own and other believers', that must have been whispered throughout that time in his life. On both pages he drew three connected crosses. The very next entry was a draft of an exciting fictional story about an eerie room—Spiders! Thunder! Chainsaws!— followed by his list of possible topics for his lemon and lemonade narratives. That list included twinned topics of losing his biological parents and having his foster parents in his life, and missing his brothers and knowing he'll get to visit them, as well as getting lots of shots for his illness, which is the one lemon topic without a sweeter counterpoint.

In an entry nestled between his list of possible topics and some stories more directly about his cancer, Carlton wrote about his grandfather's death: "I was very sad the day my grandpa died and they drove him away in a limo. He died almost 4 years ago. I even go visit his grave and I tell God I wish he had a second chance to live because he meant a lot to me and I love him so much." For any child, writing about the loss of a grandparent is significant, but for Carlton, whose illness meant the idea of death was hovering in a close and personal way, pleading with God for second chances resonates particularly deeply. And his story about his grandfather is set in a time in his life when he lived with his biological family, a setting that can't help but reverberate with the additional traumas that would unfold over the coming 4 years.

Another entry jumped to the present and focused on his foster parents, who he called Aunty and Uncle. He wrote, "I am glad that I am living with my aunty and uncle because they take very good care of me and take me to school and take me to the doctor's office. And that tells me they care about me." His writing about his foster parents included the telling detail of their role in getting him to two of the central contexts of his life in 2nd grade: school and the doctor's office. For Carlton, getting to his medical appointments was literally a matter of life or death.

Although Carlton's treatment had progressed to a very hopeful point at the end of 2nd grade, he continued to experience repercussions of his illness over the next few years. Megan had grown close to the family and surely, no matter what, would have had regular updates on his illness from Carlton and his foster parents. However, our insights into Carlton's experiences were deepened through his little sister Sonia, who entered Megan's classroom 2 years after Carlton. Sonia and Carlton had been kept together when they were moved from their parents' care to their foster parents' home. The trauma of Carlton's illness was a consistent presence in Sonia's writing, as is her processing of the loss of her biological family, particularly her three older brothers (see Chapter 4 to revisit her poem about her brothers). Sonia was a prolific writer, so her notebook is filled with many more pages of writing than her brother's, but her themes echo Carlton's responses to Megan's invitations to testify through school literacies.

The theme of family, for instance, is central in Sonia's narrative "The Amazing Trip," in which she described a visit with members of her extended biological family. "One Saturday afternoon my family got a call from my dad's dad and brother and cousins," she wrote, describing how they set out on a trip to see relatives, picking up cousins along the way who didn't have a car. Like Carlton, her writing notebook entries included time jumps between her biological family and her foster parents.

Shifting to the siblings' life with their foster parents (who she calls "Mom" and "Dad"), Sonia focused several of her personal narratives on Carlton's illness. In "The Emergency Room," she wrote, "Yesterday at 3:00 pm my brother didn't feel good. So, my mom gave Carlton medicine, but he didn't feel any better. We took him to the emergency room. We were there from 9:30 to 1:30 am. Carlton had to get a needle to a tube and they touched the bump. He had an x-ray and a cat scan. Then we left."

This recounting of an emergency visit to the hospital provides a child's view of what Carlton went through on those visits. She captures the long waits, the needles, and, significantly, the doctors touching "the bump," which I imagine is the place on Carlton's chest where his portacath had been. "The bump" had to be an unsettling presence for a younger sibling and, as Carlton shared in 2nd grade, it was often painful. A doctor's probing fingers would have been a scary and dreaded experience for her big brother. This story of the frightening realities of a diagnosis that continued to visit its wrath on the only brother she still has in her daily life pairs with Sonia's poetry stanza about Carlton, where she explicitly expressed her fear of losing him.

Her writing about Carlton's illness also addressed her family's experience with the Make a Wish Foundation. In "The Exciting News," she wrote, "Last week my mom got a call from a cancer girl named Chickie. It said 'Hi. I got great news for you! Call me back!' We were excited! We called her back. . . . She said they picked our letter."

I remember the day Carlton stopped by Megan's classroom during his lunch time in 3rd grade to share this exciting news with her. He beamed as Megan whooped with joy and gave him a big hug. The Make a Wish trip to Disney World was a significant event for Sonia too, of course, and she wrote another long entry about it, filled with dialogue and detail, titled "The Cancer Trip." She wrote, "My brother had cancer. About the last day the doctor asked, 'What's your wish? Going to Disney World or Disney land. If you don't want to go to those you can pick any place.' My brother said, excited, 'Disney World!'" She vividly described the details of the journey to Florida, writing about waiting for the limo to pick them up, the airport, the flight (she had Sprite *and* hot chocolate), and picking up the rental car. Her writing was peppered with exclamations (Yay! We were excited! I could not wait any longer! We're here!). The joy of this trip was wrapped up in the trauma of Carlton's illness. His trauma was also Sonia's, the little sister witness to it all.

For our goals as teachers attending to how children respond to invitations to bring the difficult dimensions of their lives to school literacies, the siblings offer a unique and rare window into how traumas unfold over time, are shared in families, and linger in the pillar stories children bring to their literacies.

CLASSROOMS AS SITES OF SWIRLED STORIES

Sometimes, when following children's meaningful and impactful experiences across literacy units or an entire school year, it becomes clear how many given moments of testimony and witness are spun up with others. We can find ourselves in a cotton candy swirl of connections. One child's story of trauma will spin its silk lines of connection with others'.

When you take up pedagogies of testimony and critical witness in your classroom, that web of connections *is* present. We won't ever have access to all of those entwinements of testimony and witness, witness and testimony. But when a few of those interconnected threads become visible, we get to learn from them. That's what happened during a discussion of the book *Amber Was Brave, Essie Was Smart* by Vera B. Williams (2004) when Malina, Javier, Abran, Wren, Megan, and I were all present at the table.

Before we get to that discussion, it is important to meet Malina and know a bit about my connections with her in that 2nd year of our study. Malina was a keen listener who had a talent for building relationships, and from the first time we met at the start of 2nd grade, she had this way of making me feel welcome and befriended in the classroom. She was an outgoing, effervescent person, and, in addition to bringing energy to her interactions, she held eye contact in a way that made me, and I imagine others, feel seen and heard. She also had an open and forthright way of addressing hard and hurtful experiences: One day, in a discussion about the book *Tar Beach*, she shared with Megan and her classmates about anti-Black racist language that was directed at her by a White child on the playground. Her experience sparked an important discussion of racism and the children's experiences of racism in and outside of school. In that conversation and others, Malina was a child who noticed and engaged with connections between her own experiences and others', including mine.

Second grade turned out to be a momentous year for Malina. When a ballet troupe from a prestigious academy of dance in the nearby city visited the school early in the year for a performance and workshop, the leaders recognized Malina's talent and started conversations with Megan and Malina's mother about getting Malina involved in the ballet school. Tuition would have been impossible for Malina's mother, but the school was offering a full scholarship. The family's limited income also meant that transportation to the city was inaccessible for Malina's mother. Megan chose to push away the scolding voices that insisted involvement with families is only okay up to a point, and decided she would offer to drive Malina to her dance classes after school each Wednesday. Malina's mother accepted Megan's offer, and Malina was thrilled with her dance classes. The commutes to and from the dance school created a close bond between Malina and Megan, which was visible in the many writer's notebook entries Malina wrote about her love for her teacher.

Family was also a major presence in Malina's writing. Like many of her classmates, Malina laced her father across her stories, poems, topic lists, and letters during 2nd grade. She wrote her first narrative about her father (but far from her last) following a personal narrative mini-lesson with Woodson's *Visiting Day* as mentor text. She wrote:

> My Dad was in jail. I was sad and mad because my Dad is always being a bad Dad and I do not like it. I wish he was not a bad person. Then I would be proud of him. But I am not proud of him. I am angry at my bad Dad. That is why my mom does not let us see our Dad. The End.

She expressed her anger at her father, wrapped up in her sadness, and her wish that he could be a parent worthy of her pride. Her response to the invitation Megan opened for connection to Woodson's book provided a context for those complex feelings about her father. And, looking across the year, Malina brought a spectrum of father-feelings to the page. Drafting a poem about love, she wrote, "Love is true. Love is here. I love my Dad. I love my Mom. I love my family." When writing a list of facts about herself, "I have one Dad" was listed right after where she was born, when she was born, and "I have two sisters." Her father hovered as a presence in a letter to her sister who, she explained, is "the one I had never seen." She explained that she was just a baby and "My dad was really bad and my mom had broken up with him because he was really bad and that was when I wasn't able to see my sister anymore." In another entry in her writer's notebook, she wrote that her mom loved her so much "she can break out of a cell," underscoring the threat of bars to separate parents and children.

Malina was a model of reciprocal witnessing. She brought a spark of delight, perfectly coupled with empathy, when she responded with heart-full curiosity to my mention, in one of our early conversations about writing, of my own family experience with incarceration. Once we discovered this overlap of experience (with, of course, *starkly* different stakes and consequences), she often sought conversations about her father, my brother, and our writing about them. All of this occurred before the discussion of *Amber Was Brave, Essie Was Smart* and serves as an important backdrop to the web of testimony and witness that spun in that conversation. I also invite you to revisit Abran's and Wren's letters, written to the fathers they'd lost, that I shared in Chapter 4, as having them close in mind will also be helpful in what follows.

One day in spring, Malina and her three classmates were reading *Amber Was Brave, Essie Was Smart* as part of their "Lunch Bunch" literature discussion group with Megan. Megan formed the group as part of a children's literature project she needed to complete for a graduate course that asked teachers to plan and enact an experience with literature that the teacher would define as socially and culturally relevant for students. Megan chose to focus on themes of poverty, loss, peace, and race and racism. Because it was so connected to the goals of our inquiry, we decided to fold it into our study of pedagogies of testimony and critical witness in her classroom.

In *Amber Was Brave, Essie Was Smart*, which is written as a series of poems, someone asks the two titular sisters, "Where is your dad?" It is "The question that always made Amber cry." This is how readers first learn that the father is absent, but they don't yet know why. Although it is soon revealed that the father is in jail after being convicted of check fraud, at the point when the cause of absence is not yet known, it is just father loss, in all its forms, that filled the Lunch Bunch space. As the speculations began about why the father might be gone and where he might be now, I felt the presence of this particular absence and how I knew it connected to some of the children's experiences.

Abran said, "I think their dad passed away and they can't forget about it and they keep talking and it makes them cry. They think about all the fun times she had with her dad and now he's gone."

Wren followed with her own prediction, saying, "I think I know too. I think their dad was really mean to them and sometimes they think about what it would be like to have a dad who would be really nice and they ask their mom for another dad and she probably says yes, but she can't find a dad who is nice."

I have to pause here, close my eyes, and let myself dissolve into the losses and longings that enveloped these predictions. We know that Abran's own father had died 2 years earlier. His writing and talk about his father across 2nd grade was full of fun times they had together and the punctuated suddenness of "now he's gone." And Wren's father? We can recall from her letter to him that he died when she was an infant and became a wistful, literally angelic presence in her writing. As Wren shared with me that year in conversations and in her writing, her mother had brought a few different boyfriends into the home over time. None of them, she told me, were nice.

Other children had predictions too, and they all wanted to discover why that father was gone. Megan affirmed the children's ideas and continued to read, stopping after the poem that holds the reveal. The father was in prison. My eyes went straight to Malina. Her eyes widened as she sat up straighter and bounced a little in her chair. She immediately looked over, caught my eye, and gave me a small smile. We shared a nod of recognition as Megan closed the book, thanked the children, and told them she was so glad they'd get to continue their discussions soon.

The next day, as all settled at the kidney-shaped table and opened their cardboard cartons of milk, Malina volunteered to summarize what the group had read and discussed the day before.

Malina: "We met Essie and Amber and the part we stopped at was they were remembering that their dad went to jail because he wrote a fake check. And she [pointing to me] has a connection. She remembers her brother did that too."

Megan: "She does. Did she share that with you?"

Malina: "Uh huh."

Megan: "Wow. That's a powerful connection. Thank you for sharing, Ms. Elizabeth."

Me: "So, I had shared my connection that my brother also went to jail."

Megan: "Do you want to share that with us, with the whole group?"

Me: "Sure. Because in small moments Malina had a small moment and I was connecting that my brother also went to jail. He's been out of jail for 2 years and he was in jail for a long time. So we were remembering the moment when we heard that people in our lives were going to jail and it's a connection to this book too."

Megan: "Thanks for remembering that."

Sherri: "I remember my connection that, um, Otis in *Winn-Dixie* went to jail just like the dad."

Javier: "I have a connection too." (He says this as Sherri begins to talk. She initially gets the floor.)

Javier: [louder] "I have a connection too, because my dad was in jail."

Megan: "He was. But he's home now, isn't he? And that was an idea that you said, Javier—that you could have, you could write a small moment about it."

Javier nods.

I can freeze the video right at the moment on that first day when the poem line lands and Malina suddenly seems to sit higher in her chair, eyes about to turn to mine; and again the moment a day later when Javier gets his words in edgewise and he shares this experience for the first time in front of his peers, his face reflecting whatever would be the opposite of trepidation. From that moment on his father became more present in his writer's notebook.

In addition to showing how testimony and witness spread across children's and adults' experiences in classrooms, this discussion at the Lunch Bunch table illustrates key principles of critical witnessing. Serving as a critical witness to children happens in the moment-to-moment of classrooms, but it also requires inquiry and investigation into the rich and layered ways children bring their lived knowledge to their literacies.

To take an example relevant to the Lunch Bunch discussion, schools and the wider society are saturated with racialized and classed assumptions about absent or inattentive fathers that are consistently told and circulated through the media, popular culture, and political rhetoric and imagery. When a child of color or a child experiencing economic struggle writes of incarcerated fathers, those stories can too often be absorbed and retold in ways that reinforce harmful and consequential assumptions and ignore the realities of racism built into the policies and practices of law enforcement. When a White, upper-middle-class child writes a parallel story, it is more likely to be met with sympathy and viewed as an exception to an assumed norm of loving and present parents. It takes intention and commitment to recognize, resist, and challenge those destructive, wounding myths.

Challenging those kinds of harmful narratives in their various forms should not fall only on teachers whose identities make them targets of the toxicity of those false stories. Each of us can and must recognize marginalizing language and beliefs when they arise, shift our own assumptions to any extent needed, and speak out in solidarity with children, families, and colleagues. And we can enact those commitments while also being moved by children's testimonies and their remarkable capacity to serve as witnesses to others' lives.

REFLECTIONS ON TRACING TESTIMONY AND WITNESS ACROSS TIME

Immersing myself in the literacies and lives of the children in Megan's classroom, I can feel the gentle wrap of the spring-green vines of the testimonies and acts of witnessing from across each school year. I feel the tug of those tendrils—from Woodson's *Visiting Day*, to Malina, to *Amber Was Brave, Essie Was Smart*, to me, to Javier. I sense them winding from Abran's and Wren's text predictions back to their letters to their dads and their talk about what writing about their dads meant to them that year. I become more attuned to when Miguel is present in Enrique's writing, long before the adored big cousin's physical absence is ever put on the page. I follow the proliferating father-writing across the weeks, months, and years and let the presence of pets help me understand how some lucky children, as yet spared some of the hardships of their peers, are absorbing and processing the unpredictable ways life imposes loss, frustration, and grief. I see the depth of insight and understanding about injustices inside and outside of schools that many children bring to their school literacies.

We will not hear or know about all of the lived knowledge, the connections and disconnections, that will follow from enacting pedagogies of testimony and witness in our classroom. Silence, as Schultz (2009) reminds us, is chock-full of complexities, brimming over with stories, and always connected to children's rich knowledge and histories. But we *will* encounter, in various forms, children's testimony to the challenges of their lives and their witnessing of your life and their peers'.

We can't leave those encounters with children's difficult experiences to chance. One concrete action you can take immediately is to begin reading your students' writing for threads across time. This can include children's work and talk in the writing portion of your literacy block and in the various forms of children's response to their reading. As I've argued here, to access the richness of children's responses to mindful inclusion of testimony and witness to trauma, we need to immerse ourselves in children's literacies in at least two ways:

- Tracing how particular life experiences, including trauma, may arise in explicit and implicit ways within individual children's writing (within and across genres and units of study and the formal and informal spaces of school).
- Attuning to how testimony and witness of your own and their peers' challenging life experiences connect to children's folding of trauma into school literacies.

We know that spending time with students' work is central to a deep understanding of what children know and how we can best support their learning. Those are the rich processes of learning from children that we call "formative assessment." For our purposes, we get to take up that process with additional goals, centered on children's humanity as well as our own—the shared vulnerabilities of being human, and the ways that some bodies, more than others, are impacted by oppression.

To run with the vine metaphor (because, why not?), I hope this chapter shows that when trauma is invited as a source of knowledge and resource for school literacies, the winding tentacles of life will climb every wall, fill every corner, wrap their tender shoots around one ankle, another wrist, and spread to the spine of that book on the shelf. We don't have to see each connection to know they are there, but by paying mindful, intentional attention we can get glimpses and picture-window views of how children draw on the fullness of their lives to nurture their own and others' literacies and learning. Let's let those sightings fuel our commitments.

FOR REFLECTION, DISCUSSION, AND PRACTICE

- Identify an upcoming literacy unit and read through children's work for connections that arise across your classroom. What do you notice about what children are engaging and investing in through their writing? What potential connections do you see between children's writing and the talk and testimony that you or their peers have shared? How does children's writing invite you to zoom in or zoom out to see the big ideas and life knowledge at play in children's writing? What do you see emerge as you read students' work in this way?

- Think of two or three children whose experiences in literacy over time you are most compelled to better understand. Spend time with one child's literacy work across time and instructional contexts. What do you notice in that child's work over time? What are their topics, the forms their writing takes, and their use of language? What does their presence on the page suggest to you over time? And what does "absence" or silence on some activities and spaces also tell you? Do you see threads of connection you hadn't noticed before?

- Take one week to deliberately attune to how children are positioned through language in and beyond your school. What labels do you hear used to refer to children? These can range of course from academic labels such as "high" and "low" to labels about children and families such as "broken" or "at risk." What do you notice about how language works to separate groups of people (in other words, forms of us/them language, such as "those families" or "that population")? Then invite trusted colleagues (or friends outside of school, or, if necessary, turn to your private journaling) to discuss what you've noticed. Come up with ways to productively resist such language when you hear it (what, specifically, might you say in response?). Work to generate more positive and asset-based language to replace the harmful labels and shift us/them language.

CHAPTER 6

Conclusion

How My Heart Explodes
The day
she passed away
my heart exploded
into little pieces.
Her name was written
all over my heart.
I just can't believe
my heart exploded.
How can anyone survive
their heart exploding?
—Tiana

What does trauma *do* in literacy classrooms? I cannot capture my response to Tiana's poem on this page, with my fingers clicking across these plastic keys with their limited set of symbols. You can't crawl into my flesh, my memory, the stories that live in my bones. Tiana's poem shakes those stories loose. It is hers, this collection of lines, but she ushers her readers in. This heart-exploding loss speaks, no doubt, to the depths of your own missing. Her poem, like all great writing, is an invitation to be pulled into the author's imagination and to catch glimpses of yourself. Who and what do you see mirrored back as you peer into your own eyes?

Tiana was grieving her baby sister, a fleeting physical presence who will be a present-absence for a lifetime. Her grief, like other children's pain, like yours, may become less sharp over time, or be rawer on some days more than others. But the most difficult aspects of life will always be part of who a person is, essential to the knowing they bring to the world and how it works. It is a world never fair, never easy. It is a world in which humans find ways to inflict extra trauma on some people more than others. And it is a world full of meaning-seeking, love-wishing, and pursuit of being seen in the full complexity of being human.

Amidst the accumulating conversations about trauma and schools, this book has focused on how difficult experiences, of whatever source and kind, can and must be viewed as integral to classroom literacies. Difficult experiences have been and will evermore be present in the lives of children entering schools. In the literacies and lives shared in classrooms, a goal to honor trauma—to feel and feel deeply, to attune to encounters with children's lives, to be the witnesses they deserve—is desirable. It is necessary. It is possible. It is also perilous. Centering trauma as powerful pedagogy in classrooms is all of those things.

Expressions of loss, pain, yearning, and struggle require pulling others' stories into the heart and soul of shared humanity *and* require space to recognize the distinctions in experiences and what accounts for those differences. We *can* hold both of these necessities—embrace and distance—in our heads, hearts, and actions at the same time. It is not one or the other. It is both, all the time.

Tiana's poem can help us challenge another false opposition that arises in conversations about trauma and schools. Labeling adults as the healers and children as the wounded is unnecessary, unproductive, and, well, simply wrong. Sometimes those assumptions about who is damaged and who is whole are implicit and, other times, quite explicit. Children on whom life has inflicted more hardship than anyone should have to bear should not be further weighed down with those heaviest of labels. Children should not be visually and symbolically crowded into the lowest levels of someone's idea of a hierarchy of wellness and actualized humanity. So when we see representations of trauma that reserve cognitive and emotional vibrancy for those blessed with the most material and social comforts our systems can afford, we need to have our side-eye ready.

Because as educators we know better, don't we? Spending time with children, talking with them, listening to them, reading their writing, I'm knocked sideways by their wisdom. The children's words I've shared in these chapters represent a slice of the knowledge that children hold and the evocative ways that they convey their pursuit of meaning and connection through all that life may bring. Children have knowledge of aspects of life and humanity and inhumanity that I will never, can never, have. Our knowledge of children and their capacity for drawing on their own lives as a resource for learning must lead us to question any approaches to trauma that insist on separating teachers and children; that presume to help "us" better understand "them."

To turn again to a metaphor I used in Chapter 1, I remind myself here and at every turn: Children are not fragile, newly hatched chicks, and we, their teachers, are not just strong hands capable of so much care and so much harm. It is the life stories in classrooms that a community of children and adults can step forward, hands cupped and ready, to gently hold for one another.

LIVING THE TENETS OF TESTIMONY AND CRITICAL WITNESS

Approaching trauma through pedagogies of testimony and critical witness is a courageous and necessary commitment. As I've emphasized throughout these pages, honoring and embracing trauma as part of classroom life, love, and connection is risky teaching. It is *far* riskier, though, to implicitly or explicitly require children to leave crucial life experiences at the classroom door. And that is what we do, what curriculum does, no matter how good the intentions, when we only model safe, easy topics or steer students to more comfortable ground when they raise the hard stuff of life. We can ensure that children have space and flexibility to engage their full lives in their literacies in ways that work for *them*.

As a reminder, here are the three central tenets of the pedagogies of testimony and critical witness (the detailed descriptions are in Chapter 2):

- Testimony and Witness Are Reciprocal
- Critical Witness Requires Action and Advocacy
- Testimony and Critical Witness to Trauma Are Woven into the Fabric of School Literacies.

With these principles in mind, I revisit some central ideas from this book that you may be mulling over as you look toward your own commitments and classroom practice.

Questioning "Trauma" and What Counts as Traumatic

"Trauma" is both the weightiest and flightiest of terms—heavy with the certainty of hurt, loss, pain, despair, violence, yet afloat on a breeze of ambiguity of meaning and implications. To revisit a key idea discussed in Chapter 1, the meaning of the word "trauma" can't be taken as a given, even as we see it used in trauma-informed policies as if its meaning is clear. Because attaching trauma to children's lives is so consequential, it is useful to resist arriving in classrooms with clear or fixed definitions of what trauma *is*. Instead, as illustrated in the previous chapters, we can turn our questions toward the lived circumstances and consequences of how difficult life experiences circulate in classrooms. And we can pursue the pedagogies necessary if children are to have opportunities to draw on all dimensions of their lives as source and resource for their literacy learning.

Providing Invitations, But Never Requirements

Although Megan and the other teachers that we've encountered in this book modeled for students that revealing the hardest times of life and writing about deeply felt experiences was possible and would be supported in the classroom, children always had choices about whether and how to share their stories. Whether it is the literal pain of chemotherapy treatments, the deep emotional hurt of separation from loved ones, the confusion of ever-shifting shelter, the fear over what those flashing lights portend, or the worry that a lost dog will never be found, these literacy pedagogies offer an explicit invitation and endorsement of all aspects of children's lives.

The shape of the invitations that you provide to children will shift, for sure, depending on the stories that enter the room in any given year or class. Prior to meeting Carlton, Megan had first encountered the power of allowing her students to serve as witnesses to her own challenges and of using those empathic connections to fuel their own writing. However, her commitments to pedagogies of testimony and critical witness became all the more salient when Carlton entered her classroom.

Forms of the invitations that you provide will also vary from genre to genre, instructional goal to instructional goal. The literacy curriculum may determine the order of units, the flow and timing of your lessons, or the central texts that you introduce. And for many of you, the curriculum may also specify questions that you must ask and the sentence frames, graphic organizers, or rubrics that you're expected to include (at least some of which I'm hopeful will be rich and useful tools for your teaching).

However, no curriculum can dictate your own lived stories—the treasure trove of your own connections between literacy and your most meaningful memories and moments. When you testify to your connections to texts, genres, and topics, some children will feel a spark of recognition and find their routes to making those literacy contexts count for their pillar life experiences. The invitation, your testimony, opens a door. Each child, though, gets to decide whether, when, and how they enter.

Drawing on Rich and Relevant Mentor Texts

Across genres, the mentor texts that we use matter. Those mentor texts are often a teacher's own testimony to something deeply meaningful—including trauma, in whatever form that takes. Teachers also draw on published authors' texts that connect with their knowledge of children's lives. As we saw in earlier chapters, sometimes, for some children, connections with a teacher's or other author's shared experience may come in the specifics—the death of a loved one, a family member's incarceration, too-few financial resources, or the longing for family across national borders. As we also saw, sometimes opportunities for connection arise in the larger themes in your and other authors' writing—loss, fear, courage, outrage, grief, or confusion.

Critical witness of children's lives is crucial in relation to mentor texts, as it is in all instructional decisions related to trauma. We can imagine (with horror!) the ways someone could use unfounded and deficit-fueled assumptions about children to select mentor texts. In building pedagogies of testimony and critical witness, the spirit and commitments we bring to our teaching matter just as much as the texts themselves.

Letting Go of Trauma Hierarchies

It simply makes sense that certain of our life stories are most formative and core to who we are. When they are important to us, the ways they matter can be witnessed by others. Still, as I discussed in Chapter 2, teachers often express concern that they don't have "enough" challenge in life to engage in vulnerable testimony with children and position students as witnesses. Raising those questions about our own experiences relative to children's is an important impulse, even as we must challenge it. For many teachers, that self-questioning reflects a critical sense of the social and economic privileges that have shielded them from traumas inflicted by social systems and institutions. Questioning your right to share your life's challenges can signal that you are being careful not to appropriate or overidentify with others' lives and the challenges they have faced.

However, we can't let those questions turn to fear and silence. *No one gets through life unscathed.* And it is clear from watching children respond to teachers' testimonies that a teacher's story offers powerful invitations to children to weave their own most pressing experiences through their literacies across a school year. We saw this unfold multiple times in Megan's classroom as she drew on experiences that, though very hard and truly sorrowful, did not approach the trauma of some of the children in her classroom. Yet, over and over, children served as empathetic witnesses and made their own connections and decisions about how they might take up difficult dimensions of their lives in their literacies.

Being Intentional and Being Authentic

I have no doubt that you already think about and feel the ways intention, authenticity, and spontaneity are melded in literacy instruction. This happens through the delight you feel when a student shares a unique idea in a discussion, the giggles that teachers and children share as a read-aloud unfolds or a chart falls off the wall, or the way a child's insightful question reshapes a lesson in rich and unexpected ways. When we bring trauma into the scene, though, we often need to explicitly re-embrace how mindful planning and our authentic feelings and vulnerabilities can co-exist in our teaching.

The lessons we plan for opportunities for testimony and witness will connect in visceral ways to the experiences we invite children to witness. In Chapter 4 we saw an example of this when Megan planned a poetry writing lesson that connected to her experience of getting choked up reading

Because of Winn-Dixie during read-aloud the previous day. In other words, intentionality and authenticity are synchronous in our use of testimony to invite children to bring hard experiences to literacies. In my own teaching, I often share the loss of my little brother in highly intentional ways. I testify to my loss as a source of connection and as an invitation for students to bring to our university classroom who we are and the stories we carry. It doesn't matter how many times I tell it, though—my voice and hands always quiver a bit. Sharing the hard stuff always makes us vulnerable.

Related to this is how planning a lesson as invitation to bring trauma to school literacies can and will also address curricular goals. My hope is that these stories from classrooms challenge any either/or notions that we may hold related to spontaneous connection with others' stories *versus* planning instructional contexts that allow for those connections to occur. In Megan's instruction, we saw her make specific moves in her talk and actions to position children as witnesses to a challenging experience from her life. And, at the same time, she also continually and explicitly modeled and centered the literacy processes and skills of the lesson.

Centering Trauma Includes Centering Joy

Throughout this book, children have shown us how centering trauma as powerful pedagogy means recognizing how pain and joy, loss and connection, are wrapped up in one another. Tiana beamed with pride as she shared her poem of impossible heartache. Carlton eagerly pulled up his shirt to show his portacath to his classmates and describe how it worked to help him fight his disease. Malina was bursting to share the connections she'd so attentively woven between some of us at the back table and the characters in the book she and her classmates were discussing.

The joy amidst trauma arrives in connections with others, in risking vulnerability, in opportunities to see and absorb children's capacities for empathy and compassion, in experiencing how a child's investment ignites when bringing the depths of life to school literacies, in resisting messages of broken and damaged children, and in attuning to the moment-to-moment and year-to-year pursuit of our most heartfelt commitments.

Recognizing the Political and Personal Stakes of Trauma

Because trauma for children is multipronged, addressing trauma in schools is always both personal *and* political. As we recognize and embrace the hard experiences of children's lives as resources for school literacies, teachers can support one another to keep the stakes of those efforts in view. As I've emphasized, the stakes are high with trauma, because the language and framing of children's trauma can be yet another source of marginalization for some children.

We see time and again how difficulties children face are interpreted through the double-edged sword of rejection and pity. Stephanie Jones (2004), for instance, describes how a child shared "my dad is a bully" during a literacy discussion about bullying. Her teacher, clearly uncomfortable, ignored her contribution. Indeed, literacy research from K–12 classrooms offers countless examples of students being silenced when they raise important experiences from their lives, often embedded in issues of racism, economic inequality, sexism, and gender policing and homophobia. Such shutting-down of children's knowledge and personhood is one way that school has too often inflicted additional trauma on students.

Literacy teachers can be powerful leaders in insisting on compassionate *and* critical approaches to trauma in schools. We can help ourselves and colleagues recognize how political engagement and a sharp analytic eye are inextricably linked to loving, relational, and humanizing classrooms. As trauma moves to the center of many conversations in education, teachers like you are poised to raise the questions, voice the challenges, and be the needed change.

TEACHERS' WELL-BEING IN THE MIDST OF COMMITMENT

It is crucial to turn the lens toward your own well-being as you take up this important, feeling-drenched work in your literacy classroom. It would take another book to delve adequately into teachers' perspectives on crafting their classrooms as spaces where reciprocal vulnerability, testimony, and witness are present for them and for students. However, I turn briefly here to teachers' voices to emphasize how teachers have spoken to living their commitments.

In my conversations with teacher colleagues, they often used identity-focused language to talk about their take-up of these kinds of pedagogies. Kristen, for instance, shared, "I can't imagine teaching without it . . . that is such an integral part of my teaching. I can't imagine just walking into a class and not having a relationship with them, where they would know that I would be okay with them talking to me about anything." Like her colleagues in our inquiry group, Kristen sees relationship, vulnerability, and reciprocity as central to who she is as a teacher.

Megan spoke to confronting the risks of vulnerability in her teaching, saying, "It's scary to make yourself vulnerable, but yet, with whatever we're asking students to do, whether it's a 'happy' story or not, we're still asking them to probe deeper into their own lives, and share that out, and so we should be able to do that too." Although she sees vulnerable teaching as crucial, she also acknowledges the complexities of feeling that come with those commitments. As she described, "My head is spinning, but at the same time I feel a strange sense of peace with the genuine nature of the work I am doing with my students. Yes, it is overwhelming. Yes, it raises a tremendous number of questions. But it is important and I will keep pushing myself."

Teachers also described the importance of taking care of themselves as they deeply invest in children's lives. As Megan put it, "It's dealing with things that these children cannot control, and, you know, you need to find a way, to leave it. But that's not who I am. So it's not really finding a way to *leave* it. It's more about finding a way to manage it and accept what I'm doing." Similarly, Marie explained that the word "boundaries" didn't capture the realities of her work with children. But, she emphasized, "devoting time to the parts of life outside of teaching that really fuel me is so important— and it takes attention to do that. It doesn't just happen."

Teachers also shared how approaching difficult experiences with intention propelled their commitments to strive toward justice in educational institutions, policies, and practices. Victoria, a 5th-grade teacher, talked about her commitment to support a child who had recently entered her classroom and whose traumas and "behavior issues" had been circulating in her school.

> When Jack came in I kept hearing all these stories about him, and oh my god, and crazy Jack, and you know, all of this stuff. I thought, this is so sad. Why do teachers do that? Why do they pass on something? Why don't we just let kids have a clean, fresh, start? Maybe he's ready to start new. I told him, I said, it's a whole new start right here. I said, I don't know what is in your record from before. I didn't read it. I don't care to read it.

For teachers who have invested in pedagogies that invite the complexities of life into classrooms, who infuse their teaching with heart and respect, and who see themselves as advocates for children within and beyond school walls, there is a sense of no turning back. As Megan described, she has students whose families faced deportation, racial profiling, and the multiple impacts of economic insecurity. "How can classrooms not allow for the important parts of life to come in? I mean, I'm just fascinated to go into a classroom where that doesn't exist. What does that even look like?"

SEEKING CONNECTION AND COLLABORATION

I know that flexibility and opportunity in our teaching can vary greatly across school contexts. The variation in literacy curricula across states and districts is always striking, and I have talked with plenty of teachers who are discouraged or disallowed from spending instructional time on certain genres. Others are teaching tightly scripted curricula, with a lot of oversight and without any sense of wiggle room. If you're in that situation, wishing your curriculum included more space for the practices and pedagogies I've discussed, it is well worth lobbying for change. But you shouldn't have to do it alone.

One of the potentially productive and hopeful aspects of attention to children's trauma moving to the forefront of discussion in education is that administrators and policymakers are paying attention to this area of research and practice. Such attention can open doors for conversations about curricular and instructional contexts for supporting students facing life challenges. In pursuit of those conversations, connect with colleagues with similar goals and commitments and reach out to trusted local school leaders who can help you strategize and craft your argument. And if I can support your efforts, please be in touch through the book's website (elizabethdutro.com).

Our individual efforts are impactful—and, whenever possible, we can seek greater impact through collaboration and coalition with colleagues, whether local or through networks that connect us across many miles. So as we work to center trauma as powerful pedagogy—to shift our practice, to embrace the vulnerability it requires to be reciprocal witnesses with our students, and to double down on our commitments to justice, equity, and advocacy—let's build a supportive community together.

EMBRACING PROCESS IN
CENTERING TRAUMA AS POWERFUL PEDAGOGY

I know what I write in this book is optimistic. My optimism is fueled by classroom inquiries with teachers and children that demonstrate how intentional, reciprocal testimony and critical witness to the hardest parts of life can stoke deeper relationships with school literacies, nurture community in classrooms, and support us in striving to be the teachers that children deserve and need us to be.

That word "strive" is crucial in relation to making trauma count for children in ways that don't cause further harm. To strive is to be focused on process, not product. Focusing on process is a principle I try to cling to in life, and I often turn to three quotes from three very different texts to help me keep process in view.

First, I turn to Gloria Anzaldúa's (1983) reminder, "Voyager, there are no bridges. We build them as we walk." Seek a bridge that has been built before you arrive at the chasm, the rushing waters, and you will inevitably spend a lot of time wandering on the side you're already on, feeling defeated and hopeless to continue the journey. Build the bridge now and know that the necessity of bridge-building is not extraordinary, not a one-time construction project; it is integral to what it means to walk.

Second, I often think about a quote from *Game of Thrones*—the TV show, not the novels, though it's probably in the novels. "Only the ladder is real," the character Littlefinger says as part of a much longer soliloquy. The entire quote holds some interesting ideas to chew over, but all I needed to take away was that image of the ladder leading to nothing. Only the ladder, stretching, in my imagination, into a fluffy cloud-filled bright blue sky. (Yes, I did turn it into a meme to share with preservice teacher colleagues.) There's no promised land endpoint at the top, no Utopia in which justice prevails and the work of striving toward more humane, connected teaching is accomplished. There is just one rung after the other, step after important step—just steady and steadfast movement.

On that point, I turn to my third inspiration to be in the process. After reading the philosophers Deleuze and Guattari's (1987) book, *A Thousand Plateaus*, I began to tell myself to "Be like the ant." Consider the ant, they urge. Ants build tunnels and carry bits of nourishment to their elaborate hills. That is what they do. When a human foot purposely or inadvertently steps on or near their hill and the tunnel collapses, we don't imagine they are shaking their little legs in frustration, lamenting their wasted efforts, swearing in whatever way an ant would curse their rotten luck. Those that survive keep making tunnels and pathways through the earth. Those tunnels will be traveled by their fellow ants, and when the next cave-in occurs, they will all take a tiny piece of the earth in their mandibles and piece by piece keep tunneling. Giving up is not in the ant's realm of possibility. It is not discouraging, not in the least, to be on that ladder, building those bridges, tunneling our way through. It's the way it is—the need to build, the potential of movement, the opportunity to rebuild.

Will we berate ourselves for moments when we know we messed up or missed something important related to our responses to trauma that a child brings to our classrooms? Will we feel it in our gut when we sense our school exacerbating a child's pain? Yep, we will. We will get frustrated and angry with colleagues who we believe are doing harm through words and actions. We will feel at sea. We will struggle with our own stories, the pains and losses that have come before and that lie ahead. We will be overwhelmed with the demands of our lives. We will despair over what fills our screens, our earbuds, our daily observations about the unconscionable injustices being inflicted on children, families, and communities. Those injustices will send us reeling. And for some reading these pages, the impacts of those piercing policies and oppressive systems are lived in your own life each and every day. For others, like me, who have retreat rights into racial, class, gender, heterosexual, gender-normative, body-able privileges—all or some of the above—we will want to be allies to children, to families, to colleagues. And we'll know we had better pay attention to and act on that lurking sense that we can always do better.

All of those complexities of feeling and of process in approaching trauma in literacy classrooms are far from the opposite of optimism and hope. We are not pursuing an ever-out-of-reach height of finally getting it right, finally finding *the* solution. There is no glorious and shining goal of perfection that we are somehow missing. We get to focus on the *process* of making hard times matter to school literacies. We get to focus on our own journey of building repertoires of questioning, reframing, and resisting frameworks and metaphors about trauma that encourage us to see children as damaged. We get to turn to the day-to-day, unit-to-unit, genre-to-genre, lesson-to-lesson decisions and moves that we can make tomorrow, next week, next month to make our classrooms vibrant, empathic spaces of testimony and witness to the fullness of the lives that enter our classrooms. We get to strive toward literacies of connection, of love, and of respect for the knowledge that comes from pain, from struggle, and toward the power of bringing that knowledge to learning. We get to fuel those commitments through the life-tilting, evocative, accomplished ways that children respond to invitations to bring life to literacies. For all of those reasons, the *process* of centering trauma as powerful pedagogy is a hopeful, optimistic, and fulfilling place to be.

A CODA—AND FINAL SUGGESTION
FOR REFLECTION, DISCUSSION, AND PRACTICE

I don't know about you, but I have these moments when I'm flooded with what life holds. And because that rush of sensations is well beyond my capacity to hold, it brims and spills over. Take last year, when I was sitting in a beyond luckily-won lottery ticket seat (literally) in a darkened theater, the curtains parted, the touring company of *Hamilton* began to sing those first few notes, and tears sprung to my eyes. It's the same with anytime the *Star Wars* soundtrack begins at the start of any of those movies (yes, even *Phantom Menace*). It's not just plays, not just movies, of course. A few months ago, I was in my car listening to a Spotify-generated playlist of 1980s pop, singing loudly to The Go-Gos' "Our Lips Are Sealed" and suddenly my voice cracks and a sob escapes. Same with Mariah Carey's "All I Want for Christmas," when I hold my baby niece and dance with her around the living room. And I always have to shift from loud chanting to silent mouthing of slogans at progressive political protests and rallies—because I am overwhelmed by the sea of humanity standing together in common cause.

Those are just the easiest-to-name moments, the ones that are bookmarked in my memory or stand in for the many, many others. Tears are often my go-to and yours may be different. So often I hear emotions, tears in this case, being labeled as "happy tears," as opposed to sad tears. To be honest, I had written the words "they were happy tears" in the sentence mentioning *Hamilton* above and then paused and quickly hit the backspace until those words were gone. I knew that was not right. When tears streamed to the Go-Gos, a song that always makes me dance in my car seat, it's not because I'm happy or because I'm sad. It's the full flood. It's all of my life in 1983 and all the years since. It's the very idea that music exists in the world and that notes, words, a certain throb of bass, can be so transportive. It's that the body responds in a way that can surprise me, even though it *is* me. It's nostalgia, it's memory, it's the passing of time, it's joy, it's passion, it's heartbreak, it's loss, it's hope, it's despair. It's my missing of my brother himself, and also of the vivid dreams that I used to have of him, his voice, his gestures, that just went away one day maybe 15 years ago and never came back.

Recently, I felt the sting of tears in the middle of the irresistibly upbeat "Party Like It's Your Birthday." The song played during the 3-hour drive back to my city home after 24 hours enveloped in the unconditional love hug of aunts, uncles, and cousins on a quick trip to that little root-town on the prairie where my mother grew up. In that moment, whatever these body-rushes mean was so tangibly intangible to me. There's no identifying all that makes up that visceral flood. But that morning I knew my cousin Justin was in there, gone to cancer at 36, his three little girls, my aunt, uncle, and cousin all infused somehow in the song's notes. And that surge of feeling is pride in my brother, who has rebuilt his life in remarkable ways and is a rock star at his factory job. It is admiration of my sister-in-law, who has found a way to pursue her teaching dreams in her rural community where kickass teachers are sorely needed. It is the hugs, kisses (in this family, we *will* kiss you on the lips, all of you, so just be aware), laughter, sense of belonging, cold pop, shot-of-whiskey-when-you-need-it-most that this family has given me all of my life and now gives to my kids. It is my now-grown-up baby sister, who propelled life forward when it felt like a dead end. It is the fact that this playlist I'm listening to was made by my daughter. It is the hope I cling to for a loved one's current journey.

Whatever form those moments take for you, we need them—as humans *and* as teachers. Committing to immersing in the harder stuff of life, for our students' sake, and for our own, means we have to recognize those moments even more intentionally and welcome them even more generously.

If it feels possible and potentially productive, I urge you to watch, listen, read, smell, gaze at the thing that invites that wave of life to wash right over you. Immerse in it, marvel at it, connect it to your teaching life, share it with your students.

Afterword

In the summer of 2017 I attended The Reading and Writing Project writing institute at Teachers College, Columbia University in New York City. An entire week dedicated to the art of teaching the writing process is joy enough for most educators, so imagine my delight when I heard echoes of the pedagogy of testimony and critical witnessing in that space. During her keynote, Professor Lucy Calkins, the founder of the Teachers College Reading and Writing Project, shared ideas that resonated with me and that I tried to capture in my notes. She said that we listen to children's stories so that they listen to their lives. She emphasized that there need to be safe places in our schools where people can be vulnerable in writing. In protecting ourselves from vulnerability, she said, we are unable to make authentic, meaningful connections with others. Indeed, as Elizabeth has so gracefully articulated throughout this book, there are moments within each and every school day that can be harnessed into transcendent opportunities that not only strengthen classroom communities, but also give children agency over their own stories and lives.

Since Elizabeth and I first began our collaboration, I have taught children across four grade levels in four vastly different educational settings. While no two school years (or days!) have been the same, one fact does remain constant: the human experience, in all of its wonderful complexity, seeps into every classroom, every day, every year. New pets, family vacations, illness, loss, injustices . . . find their way into classrooms without warning or fail.

Just this year, one of my students and his family experienced the terrifying uncertainty of a cancer diagnosis. As my student's mother went through the all-too-well-known steps of shaving her head, beginning chemotherapy treatments, and being too sick to come to school events, I thought often of Carlton and his cancer diagnosis at the beginning of 2nd grade. One day during writers workshop, I pulled out Carlton's journal from all of those years ago and put it under the document camera. My class listened in mesmerized silence as I read through his entries. My student, having watched his mother make a similar journey, used Carlton's writing as a launching pad to share his own vulnerability. That day he wrote about his mother's illness for the first time.

The work of testimony and critical witnessing is far from simple. It requires making yourself vulnerable and pushing back on the notion that certain lived experiences are, as Dmitri worried, "not for school." Katherine Paterson, a Newbery-Award winning author, also spoke during that week-long writing institute. Among other wonderful pockets of wisdom, she noted that she writes the books she does because she always wants to remember her difficult childhood experiences. Although she said she does not recall the intricate details of her childhood, she does have emotional memories of that time. She emphasized that books and writing can bind us intimately to others in ways we cannot do in our ordinary lives. My notes captured one of her beautiful metaphors: We must have chaos to give birth to a dancing star.

I would like to invite you, reader, to consider your own experiences and to breathe life into them within the walls of your classroom. You just might discover your own dancing stars.

—Megan Henning Ollett

References

Anzaldúa, G. (1983). Preface to the second edition. In C. Moraga & G. Anzaldúa (Eds.), *This bridge called my back: Writings by radical women of color* (2nd ed.; pp. iv–v). New York, NY: Kitchen Table Press.

Blackburn, M. V. (2015). *Interrupting hate: Homophobia in schools and what literacy can do about it.* New York, NY: Teachers College Press.

Blad, E. (2015, May 13). Researchers: Measures of traits like "grit" should not be used for accountability. *Education Week.* Retrieved from blogs.edweek.org/edweek/rulesforengagement/2015/05/grit_accountability_noncognitive_skills_duckworth_yeager.html

Boldt, G., Lewis, C., & Leander, K. M. (2015). Moving, feeling, desiring, teaching. *Research in the Teaching of English,49*(4), 430–435.

Bomer, K. (2010). *Hidden gems: Naming and teaching from the brilliance in every student's writing.* Portsmouth, NH: Heinemann.

Bruner, J. (1991). The narrative construction of reality. *Critical Inquiry, 18,* 1–21.

Bryant-Davis, T., & Ocampo, C. (2005). Racist incident-based trauma. *The Counseling Psychologist, 33,* 479–500.

Calkins, L., & Oxenhorn, A. (2003). *Small moments: Personal narrative writing.* Portsmouth, NH: Heinemann.

Campano, G. (2007). *Immigrant students and literacy: Reading, writing, and remembering.* New York, NY: Teachers College Press.

Campano, G., & Ghiso, M. P. (2010). Immigrant students as cosmopolitan intellectuals. In S. Wolf, K. Coats, P. Enciso, & C. Jenkins (Eds.), *The handbook of research on children's and young adult literature* (pp. 164–176). New York, NY: Routledge.

Caruth, C. (1996). *Unclaimed experience: Trauma, narrative, and history.* Baltimore, MD: Johns Hopkins University Press.

Carver, R. (2015). *All of us: The collected poems.* New York, NY: Vintage Books (Penguin).

Craig, S. E. (2015). *Trauma-sensitive schools: Learning communities transforming children's lives, K–5.* New York, NY: Teachers College Press.

Cruz, C. (2012). Making curriculum from scratch: Testimonio in an urban classroom. *Equity & Excellence in Education,45,* 460–471.

Deleuze, G., & Guattari, F. (1987). *A thousand plateaus: Capitalism and schizophrenia.* Minneapolis, MN: University of Minnesota Press.

DeNicolo, C. P., & Gonzalez, M. (2015). Testimoniando en Nepantla: Using testimonio as a pedagogical tool for exploring embodied literacies and bilingualism. *Journal of Language and Literacy Education, 11*(1), 110–126.

Duncan-Andrade, J. M. R. (2011). The principal facts: New directions in teacher education. In A. F. Ball & C. A. Tyson (Eds.), *Studying diversity in teacher education* (pp. 309–326). New York, NY: Rowman & Littlefield.

Dutro, E. (2010). What "hard times" means: Mandated curricula, middle-class assumptions, and the lives of poor children. *Research in the Teaching of English, 44,* 255–291.

Dutro, E. (2011). Writing wounded: Trauma, testimony, and critical witness in literacy classrooms. *English Education, 43,* 193–211.

Dutro, E. (2013). Toward a pedagogy of the incomprehensible: Trauma and the imperative of critical witness in literacy classrooms. *Pedagogies: An International Journal, 8,* 301–315.

Dutro, E. (2017). Let's start with heartbreak: The perilous potential of trauma in literacy classrooms. *Language Arts, 94,* 326–337.

Dutro, E., Selland, M. K., & Bien, A. C. (2013). Revealing writing, concealing writers: High-stakes assessment in an urban elementary classroom. *Journal of Literacy Research, 45,* 99–141.

Dyson, A. H. (2003). *The brothers and sisters learn to write: Popular literacies in childhood and school culture.* New York, NY: Teachers College Press.

Ellison, T. L. (2014). An African American mother's stories as TMI: MNI, ethics, and vulnerability around traumatic narratives in digital literacy research. *International Journal of Qualitative Methods, 13,* 275–292.

Fanon, F. (2008). *Black skin, white masks* (R. Philcox, Trans.). New York, NY: Grove Press.

Felman, S., & Laub, D. (1992). *Testimony: Crises of witnessing in literature, psychoanalysis, and history.* New York, NY: Routledge.

Forbes, H. (2012). *Help for Billy: A beyond consequences approach to helping challenging children in the classroom.* Boulder, CO: Beyond Consequences Institute.

Frank, A. W. (2013). *The wounded storyteller: Body, illness, and ethics.* Chicago, IL: University of Chicago Press.

Genishi, C., & Dyson, A. H. (2015). *Children, language, and literacy: Diverse learners in diverse times.* New York, NY: Teachers College Press.

Ghiso, M. P. (2016). The laundromat as the transnational local: Young children's literacies of interdependence. *Teachers College Record, 118,* 1–46.

Ghiso, M. P., & Low, D. E. (2013). Students using multimodal literacies to surface micro narratives of United States immigration. *Literacy, 47,* 26–34.

González, M. S., Plata, O., García, E., Torres, M., & Urrieta Jr., L. (2003). Testimonios de immigrantes: Students educating future teachers. *Journal of Latinos in Education, 2,* 233–243.

Gonzalez, N., Moll, L., & Amanti, C. (2005). *Funds of knowledge: Theorizing practices in households and classrooms.* New York: Lawrence Erlbaum.

Graves, D. H. (1983). *Writing: Teachers and children at work*. Exeter, NH: Heinemann.

Haberl, E. (2019). *The meaningful argument: High stakes argumentative writing and blending genre in a 7th grade classroom* (unpublished doctoral dissertation). University of Colorado Boulder, Boulder, Colorado.

Haddix, M. (2009). Black boys can write: Challenging dominant framings of African American adolescent males in literacy research. *Journal of Adolescent & Adult Literacy, 53*, 341–343.

Handsfield, L. J. (2015). *Literacy theory as practice: Connecting theory and instruction in K–12 classrooms*. New York, NY: Teachers College Press.

Handsfield, L. J., & Valente, P. (2016). Momentos de cambio: Cultivating bilingual students' epistemic privilege through memoir and testimonio. *International Journal of Multicultural Education, 18*, 138–158.

Hartman, G. (1995). On traumatic knowledge and literary studies. *New Literary History, 26*, 537–563.

Howard, T. (2017). *Relationships & learning: Keys to academic success*. Ann Arbor, MI: Teaching Works Working Papers.

Jackson, I., Sealey-Ruiz, Y., & Watson, W. (2014). Reciprocal love: Mentoring Black and Latino males through an ethos of care. *Urban Education, 49*, 394–417.

Johnson, E. (2014). Reconceptualizing vulnerability in personal narrative writing with youths. *Journal of Adolescent & Adult Literacy, 57*, 575–583.

Johnson, E., & Vasudevan, L. (2012). Seeing and hearing students' lived and embodied critical literacy practices. *Theory Into Practice, 51*, 34–41.

Johnson, L. L. (2017). The racial hauntings of one Black male professor and the disturbance of the self(ves): Self-actualization and racial storytelling as pedagogical practices. *Journal of Literacy Research, 49*, 476–502.

Jones, S. (2004). Living poverty and literacy learning: Sanctioning the topics of students' lives. *Language Arts, 81*, 461–469.

Jones, S. (2012). Trauma narratives and nomos in teacher education. *Teaching Education, 23*, 131–152.

Jones, S., & Spector, K. (2017). Becoming unstuck: Racism and misogyny as traumas diffused in the ordinary. *Language Arts, 94*, 302–312.

Jones, S., & Vagle, M. D. (2013). Living contradictions and working for change: Toward a theory of social class-sensitive pedagogy. *Educational Researcher, 42*, 129–141.

Kirkland, D. E. (2013). *A search past silence: The literacy of young Black men*. New York, NY: Teachers College Press.

LaCapra, D. (2001). *Writing history, writing trauma*. Baltimore, MD: Johns Hopkins University Press.

Ladson-Billings, G. (1994). *The dream-keepers: Successful teachers of African American students*. San Francisco, CA: Jossey-Bass.

Leander, K., & Ehret, C. (Eds.). (2019). *Affect in literacy teaching and learning: Pedagogies, politics, and coming to know*. New York, NY: Routledge.

Lewis, C. (2001). *Literary practices as social acts: Power, status, and cultural norms in the classroom*. New York, NY: Routledge.

Maranto, R. (2015). Why don't schools teach poetry? *Academic Questions, 28*, 165–174.

Miyazawa, K. (2017). Becoming co-witnesses to the Fukushima disaster in an elementary classroom. *Language Arts, 94,* 291–301.

Moraga, C., & Anzaldúa, G. (1983). *This bridge called my back: Writings by radical women of color* (2nd ed.). New York, NY: Kitchen Table Press.

Morrison, T. (2019). *The source of self-regard: Selected essays, speeches, and meditations.* New York, NY: Knopf.

Murray, D. M. (1991). All writing is autobiography. *College Composition and Communication, 42,* 66–74.

Ochs, E., & Capps, L. (2001). *Living narrative: Creating lives in everyday storytelling.* Cambridge, MA: Harvard University Press.

Olson, K. (2009). *Wounded by school: Recapturing the joy in learning and standing up to old school culture.* New York, NY: Teachers College Press.

Pacheco, M. (2009). Expansive learning and Chicana/o and Latina/o students' political historical knowledge. *Language Arts, 87,* 18–28.

Paris, D., & Alim, H. S. (Eds.). (2017). *Culturally sustaining pedagogies: Teaching and learning for justice in a changing world.* New York, NY: Teachers College Press.

Pyscher, T. (2018). A literacy of resistance: Girlhood and domestic violence. In B. J. Guzzetti, T. W. Bean, & J. Dunkerly-Bean (Eds.), *Literacies, sexualities, and gender* (pp. 57–69). New York, NY: Routledge.

Reisig, M., Bales, W., Hay, C., & Wang, X. (2007). The effect of racial inequality on black male recidivism. *Justice Quarterly, 24*(3), 408–434.

Ryan, C. L., & Hermann-Wilmarth, J. M. (2018). *Reading the rainbow: LGBTQ-inclusive literacy instruction in the elementary classroom.* New York, NY: Teachers College Press.

Saavedra, C. M. (2019). Inviting and valuing children's knowledge through testimonios: Centering literacies from within in the language arts curriculum. *Language Arts, 96,* 179–183.

Schultz, K. (2009). *Rethinking classroom participation: Listening to silent voices.* New York, NY: Teachers College Press.

Souers, K., & Hall, P. (2016). *Fostering resilient learners: Strategies for creating a trauma-sensitive classroom.* Alexandria, VA: Association for Supervision and Curriculum Development.

Souto-Manning, M., & Martell, J. (2016). *Reading, writing, and talk: Inclusive teaching strategies for diverse learners, K–2.* New York, NY: Teachers College Press.

Stoudt, B., Fine, M., & Fox, M. (2011). Growing up policed in the age of aggressive policing practices. *New York School Law Review, 56*(4), 1331–1362.

Strauss, V. (2014, April 8). Ten concerns with the "let's teach them grit" fad. *The Washington Post.* Retrieved from washingtonpost.com/news/answer-sheet/wp/2014/04/08/ten-concerns-about-the-lets-teach-them-grit-fad/?utm_term=.0f5ce60a0db4

Thein, A., & Schmidt, A. (2017). Challenging, rewarding emotion work: Critical witnessing in an afterschool book club. *Language Arts, 94,* 313–325.

Vagle, M. D., & Jones, S. (2012). The precarious nature of social class sensitivity in literacy: A social, autobiographic, and pedagogical project. *Curriculum Inquiry, 42*, 318–339.

Valenzuela, A. (2010). *Subtractive schooling: US-Mexican youth and the politics of caring.* Albany, NY: SUNY Press.

Vasquez, V. M. (2016). *Critical literacy across the K-6 curriculum.* New York, NY: Routledge.

WestEd. (2015, November 5). Trauma-informed education: Highlights of research and practice (webinar). Retrieved from wested.org/resources/trauma-informed-education/.

Winn, M. T., & Ubiles, J. R. (2011). Worthy witnessing. In A. Ball & C. Tyson (Eds.), *Studying diversity in teacher education* (pp. 295-308). New York, NY: Rowman & Littlefield.

Wissman, K., & Wiseman, A. (2011). "That's my worst nightmare": Poetry and trauma in the middle school classroom. *Pedagogies: An International Journal, 6*, 234–249.

Zembylas, M. (2008). *The politics of trauma in education.* New York, NY: Palgrave Macmillan.

Index

About the Author

Elizabeth Dutro is professor and chair of literacy studies at the University of Colorado at Boulder. Her research grew from her encounters with children, curriculum, and educational policy in her teaching in elementary schools where many families faced economic struggle and racial inequality. Starting with her PhD studies at the University of Michigan, she has collaborated with teachers and children to investigate questions about the intersections of literacy, identity, life experiences, and children's opportunities for positive, sustained, and affirming relationships with schooling. Her current studies focus on critical affective pedagogies in response to trauma and teachers' collaborative learning. Her award-winning work has been published in numerous venues, including _Journal of Literacy Research, Research in the Teaching of English, American Educational Research Journal, English Education, Teaching and Teacher Education, The Reading Teacher,_ and _Language Arts._ Elizabeth lives with her family near downtown Denver, where she can often be found drinking coffee at her favorite café, hoping you'll stop by to discuss reality TV. She can be reached at Elizabeth.dutro@ colorado.edu.